MEDITATE

A DAILY LIFE MINDFULNESS PRACTICE MANUAL

DR. THYNN THYNN

DEDICATION

This book is dedicated to my two teachers: the late Sayadaw U Eindasara and U Awthada of Burma who gave me the profound gift of Satipathana in everyday life practice and instilled in me the beginnings of a fearless spiritual wayfarer. Through their relentlessly honest, down to earth, no frills training I was able to look at myself without excuses for my failings and blind spots and also see the world without any hang ups and false expectations. To them I am deeply indebted because they gave me the herewith all to live a life of authenticity and truth.

Deep bows to their memory and kindness.

- Dr Thynn Thynn

CONTENTS

LIST of DIAGRAMS

FORWARD

For more than 20 years, Dr. Thynn Thynn has been teaching the
Daily Life Mindfulness Practice to small groups of students, first in
the living room of her home and then the library of the Sae Taw
Win II Dhamma Center she has created in Graton, California.
Reflecting on my own experience with the practice and
observations of other students, I can tell you that this is a simple,
but profound spirituality-based path to the reduction of suffering and
discontent. With this manual, Dr. Thynn Thynn is making the
practice of Mindfulness in Daily Life accessible to everyone.
While many books describing mindfulness meditation offer an
acknowledgement to the practice of mindfulness on the moments of
day to day living, which generally follows a detailed description of
sitting meditation and concentration practices, we needed an
explanation of how to actually implement the practice. This book
provides that instruction.
Dr. Thynn Thynn guides us directly into a methodical, defined
progression of learning to pay attention to every experience of the
body and mind. She offers us a process of training the mind to the
art of mindfulness in any moment; focusing on whatever is
prominent in the field of awareness; creating more wholesome
tendencies in our interactions with whatever arises internally or
externally.
The personal flavor of Dr. Thynn Thynn's style of teaching
comes through this book quite clearly. With the inclusion of
questions and answers from actual classes, one has the feeling of

sitting in that living room or library in person. You will get a true sense of how Dr. Thynn Thynn introduces us to mindfulness with loving kindness, equanimity and not without a small dash of humor. Her diagrams (especially the Cycle of Conditioning, which maps the origins of our dissatisfaction, and the exact fork in the path when we have the option of shifting perspective) clearly illustrate the text. It is hard to imagine any situation, especially any challenging situation, in life that cannot be viewed through this framework. Once seen in this way, you have already met the choice point and are on your way.

- Jane Sipe,
Sebastopol, CA 2016

--**Jane Sipe** has been a student of Dr. Thynn Thynn and the practice of Daily Life Mindfulness Practice for over 17 years. Soon after she received training from Dr Thynn in the presentation of Mindfulness practice, almost 10 years ago, she relocated to Mexico, where she was first invited to stand in for Robert Hall at one of his weekly dhamma* talks; and then was subsequently recruited to teach Daily Life Mindfulness Practice by the Dhamma Community there. With Dr. Thynn Thynn's encouragement, she led a lively and dedicated group for 4 years. In 2011, Jane returned to Sebastopol, CA where she resumed her role in the teaching program: She helped organize and teach the first STWII off-site weekend workshop: taught the Advanced Studies class; and participated in the training of two new Daily Life Mindfulness Practice teachers. She has also served on the Board of Directors of Sae Taw Win II Dhamma Foundation.

PREFACE

To most people, Buddhist meditation is synonymous with sitting cross-legged on a cushion or walking very slowly, both of which are done in silence. There is another type of meditation that is less well known: The Daily Life Mindfulness Practice. It is a powerful approach that can have real and transformative effects on day-to-day life and on how individuals perceive themselves and their relationships to the world. The Daily Life Mindfulness Practice uses some of the same disciplines and methods as silent mindfulness meditation, but it is practiced in ordinary, everyday life instead of in silent retreats. It can be practiced while working, driving, raising children, attending meetings, and negotiating conflicts, to name a few examples. In short, it can be practiced and used in all areas of life as we live it.

The Daily Life Mindfulness Practice approach was developed about fifty years ago by Burmese Buddhist monks. It is a unique practice that was not derived from tradition, but was taken directly from the suttra* on the Four Foundations of Mindfulness–the mother lode of Theravadan* Meditation.

I was fortunate to have studied in the early seventies in Burma with the two Abbots who developed the Daily Life Mindfulness Practice, Sayadaw* U Eindasara and Sayadaw U Awthada. For the past thirty years, my meditation practice has almost exclusively used this method.

I have been teaching The Daily Life Mindfulness Practice to Westerners since 1986 in Thailand and from 1991 onwards in America.

This book presents a sequence of lessons that focus on achieving mindfulness in everyday life. I developed this practice for students at the Sae Taw Win II Dhamma Center in Sebastopol, California. My students comprise a heterogeneous group from all walks of life, with individuals ranging from professionals in various fields, to housewives, photographers, students, and retirees. Many have achieved great benefits. My hope is that you too, may benefit by learning about and practicing The Daily Life Meditation Practice.

Each chapter contains didactic material explaining a particular phase of practice, followed by specific exercises pertinent to that practice, and then discussions with students about the practice. Each chapter builds on the material and experiences that arise from the exercises in the chapter before it.

For this reason, you may find it useful to read the book in sequence.

At the end of each chapter, I have included charts for you to record your experience. In this way, you can monitor your own progress when you try the practices, and also discover which areas may need more work.

I hope this book will help open doors to your inner world and bring you practical benefit in your daily life as you journey through each phase of practice and self-discovery. This practice can open doors to your inner life and lead you on a journey of immense benefit.

Thynn Thynn
Sebastopol, California

INTRODUCTION

THE MIND, NOT THE BODY

There is a popular notion that in order to meditate, we must sit in the lotus position in a quiet corner and close our eyes. People therefore tend to identify meditation with the silent sitting practice. The discipline of meditation, however, is in the training of the mind, not of the body. Our body is only an aid, or a vehicle, in which to practice mediation. This is not to, by any means, discount the silent sitting practice. Whether in the sitting or in The Daily Life Mindfulness Practice, the essence of the practice is in training the mind. In Buddhism, this means cultivating the mind in such a way that we achieve enlightenment and inner freedom. The fundamental practice is called Insight Meditation, more popularly known in the West as mindfulness meditation.

What does it mean to train the mind in the Insight Meditation system? It means training the mind to be aware of one's mind and body in a very specific way by paying attention either to the body or the mind. Don't we all know how to pay attention? Of course we do. We pay attention to our clothes, our nails, and our work. We pay attention when we read, watch TV, listen to music, go online, clean our house, cook a meal, etc. Nothing in our lives can be accomplished without paying attention to something. Then what is so special about the way we pay attention in mindfulness meditation?

In daily life mindfulness, we reverse our attention, which was previously projected outwards, and turn it inwards onto our own minds. We will learn to be more conscious of how our mind functions in everyday life when we are faced with a myriad of problems and challenges. We will begin to take care of our inner life consciously by discovering what is not working in the way that we think, feel, cling, fear, worry, love, and stress out. In other words, we will learn how to change the mental behavior patterns that cause us so much suffering. The tool we are going to use is The Daily Life Mindfulness Practice, which, in this book, I will abbreviate as DLMP.

We have been trained since we were children to pay attention to how we behave towards others; for example, to be polite and not to steal, yell, kick the dog or punch your friend. We were actually trained in our behavioral patterns to fit in with society, but we were never shown how to take care of our mind.

DLMP uses the disciplines of the Four Foundations of Mindfulness from Theravada Buddhism to integrate meditation into life itself while we are working, quarreling with our spouse, parenting, driving, or finding ourselves in the midst of conflicts and all other kinds of situations that make up our lives. DLMP is not apart from life. It is assimilated into our daily living so that we can experience life in a wholesome and balanced way. In short, it is a path to wisdom, truth and the discovery of what is best in us.

CHAPTER 1:
THE DAILY LIFE MINDFULNESS PRACTICE

Let's take a look at how we function in our daily lives before attempting to describe how to change our attention. Are you aware of how your mind is behaving in each moment? Probably not, because there are a hundred and one things competing for your attention. When you're not observing your mind consciously, then what exactly is it that you are doing? It's likely that you are moving through the day as if in a trance state. You're probably not aware of what is happening in your mind, or how much of your reactions are habitual. In short you are probably not aware of your inner life. Likely, your attention is totally absorbed in the external, and you get habitually embroiled in it.

In sitting meditation practice, the object of meditation can be fixed on whatever the meditator is using as the primary object; for instance, the breath or a mantra. But while you are going about your daily life during the waking hours, it is impossible to have one single primary object of attention throughout the whole day as you might in silent sitting. The primary object of meditation in DLMP will be whatever is most prominent in the moment through one's six senses. In daily life, the primary object of meditation will vary from moment to moment. Now you are reading. In a moment, your mind may flit to the sound of an airplane passing overhead, or to your doorbell ringing, or to an ache in your back. Your primary object has moved. If you feel an itch, then your attention may go to your itch and the itch becomes your primary object for the moment. Then you might get annoyed, and your annoyance becomes your primary object in the next moment.

The first two chapters of this book will help you learn how to be **grounded in the present moment.** The next five chapters will focus on how to develop **the quality of equanimity** of the mind through mindfulness practice. For any type of meditation, be it sitting practice or DLMP, there is a basic requirement to train the mind to be grounded in the present moment. With a mind that is running all over the place, or is too fragile, depressed, or in severe turmoil, there is very little chance for the mind to be trained in any particular manner.

Without basic groundedness, it is extremely difficult to train the mind to move on to more advanced practices that will help build the qualities of equanimity. Hence, in the beginning course series at my center, I devote three weeks to foster the mind's ability to become more stable and grounded through two primary practices:

staying in the moment, and mindfulness of peaceful mind states.

The subsequent three practices are designed to develop the quality of equanimity in the practitioner's daily life. The combination of these two approaches will bring an enormous amount of steadiness to the mind as well as a serenity and inner silence that will allow wisdom to evolve in many ways and at many levels. The end result is an inner harmony that will spill over to your outer world and also bring harmony to it.

The Mechanics of the Daily Life Mindfulness Practice (DLMP)

For those who have done a lot of silent sitting practice, here are the differences between your familiar sitting practice and DLMP.

Diagram 1.1: The Silent Sitting Meditation Model

This diagram depicts the meditator practicing silent sitting meditation. There is a zone of silence surrounding the meditator which I call the external buffer zone. This buffer keeps most of the external stimuli–noise, sight, smell, touch, and taste–at bay. The meditator is shutting down the five senses as much as possible. They may not be able to shut out everything, but at least the distracting stimuli are kept at a minimum so that the practitioner or the meditator can focus on the object of meditation.

In daily life situations, you are hit directly with sights, sounds and your own thoughts. There is no external buffer zone of silence to aid you in your meditation practice. You are at the mercy of the forces of your environment, whether they are people, objects, animals, the weather, traffic, office politics, and practically everything else. It is amidst the chaos of everyday life that you are going to learn to practice mindfulness.

How do we practice without the silence to protect us? I will give you a clue: the idea is to create your own buffer zone within yourself, in your own mind. You can't run away from noise or your spouse. You can't run away from a toothache or from bad weather. There will always be something coming at you, good or bad. There will be wonderful times, fun times and happiness, as well as pain and suffering. Everything is constantly changing, ceaselessly, like a stream. If we buckle under pressure or get knocked about in such situations, it is because our momentary samadhi (khanika samadhi*), our centering in ourselves in that moment is not strong enough, nor is our equanimity well developed to withstand what's coming at us. We instantaneously react to these impingements through our reactive mind and are thrown off balance. We are shaken up, or we descend into despair. We may stew in our anger or even worse, we may lash out at others with vengeance or recoil in passive aggression. In all these cases, we are suffering and we also make others suffer.

The mindfulness practice that I am writing about in this book is designed to help keep our mind steady and grounded in the moment, yet alert and balanced within such challenging circumstances. To become grounded we use mindfulness in the moment as our practice. We then use our practice of equanimity to help us stay alert and balanced in order to have the clarity and insight that will help us rise above the situation and handle it wisely. You may say this does not sound easy: yes, you are right, it is not. But it is not impossible. This practice is tried and true, and many have benefited from it when they learn how to persevere and be diligent in their lives.

In DLMP, our very **reactions** become our **primary objects** of mindfulness:

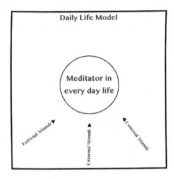

Diagram 1.2: The Daily Life Mindfulness Practice Model

We want to be aware of how we are listening to that person, how we are reacting to the bursts of energy that are thrown at us.

What is shown in the diagram is how we react normally at each moment at the point of contact with any object or event. When your reactions are tamed and become totally equanimous, then you will have created an internal buffer zone as opposed to the external buffer zone. There will be complete silence within your mind that is not dependent on what is happening outside. The outer world can be in total chaos, but internally you will be completely silent. That is the goal of The Daily Life Mindfulness Practice.

When we speak of silence, we need to answer the question, "Silence from what?" Internal silence, we'll call it "inner silence", is a silence in the absence of delusion, ill-will, and greed. Which in Buddhism we call the three roots of suffering. We watch our minds very carefully at the moment of contact with any reaction. Are we reacting with delusion, ill-will, or greed? All our commotions, all of our suffering within ourselves, occurs when these three roots or unwholesome factors arise within us at the moment of contact. That's when all the defilements or our wisdom occurs; the good and bad, they all occur in the moment of contact. It's a practice of purifying our minds. I don't like to sound too sentimental or romantic, the actual mechanism purifying the mind at each moment of contact; purifying yourself from delusion, ill-will, and greed is the mind. Ultimately, the mind that is reacting to the environment, all our own thoughts and emotions, can become completely silent from delusion, ill-will, and greed. When we are able to rest there, our mind can be in its suchness, in a completely tranquil, quiet state. Only then have we created an internal buffer where nothing in the environment can disturb the silence. Even if commotions happen, even if our mind wavers here and there, we always come back to the silence. When we are fully equanimous, that's when the best thing will happen: the arising of wisdom.

The Mundane and the Spiritual: The Dual Path

I was teaching a DLMP retreat some years ago in Australia and there was a communication gap between the organizers of the retreat and myself such that they never suspected I didn't teach sitting meditation practice.

The first evening, all the attendees were sitting like ducks in a row, then I stepped in and told them to relax and loosen up because I was not going to teach them silent sitting. For four and a half days it was total bewilderment for the attendees as they were assigned to cook, to go shopping as a group, to clean up, and to work on the grounds all along assigned to watch their minds and their reactions. It was fall in Australia and the weather was very cold. The kitchen and dining room were quite small for twenty people to be working and dining in together. Initially there was a lot of chaos and confusion. But by the third day, one of the participants, who was a minister from the United Church, said to me that he was surprised to find that his mind was still in spite of all the commotion around him. He had meditated before, but never in this way amidst the chaos of daily life.

To walk the spiritual path, you need not get away to someplace else to meditate, to retreat from this external absorption. The Daily Life Mindfulness Practice techniques teach us how to break our constant absorption in daily life affairs and experiences and to turn toward the internal activities of the mind and learn how to deal with them in such a way as to develop an internal spiritual practice that will run parallel to the external mundane life. This is what is meant by integrating the spiritual with the mundane. As the practice takes hold in your mind and becomes as natural as eating and sleeping, there will be no separation between the two worlds: the inner and outer, the spiritual and the mundane.

I have been asked many times, "Don't you ever feel the need go to retreats?" I have done only one single, four-day retreat in Burma nearly four decades ago. That's it. The Daily Life Mindfulness Practice has become second nature to me as I learned how to practice within my marriage, my family, my work life, and amidst devastating illness and disabilities. The practice is inseparable from my life, so I don't feel the need to go someplace else to develop the spiritual aspect of my life. In each moment, the mundane serves as the focus to develop the spiritual. In each moment we have an opportunity to transcend our defilements like ill-will, greed, and delusion. And it is also in each moment that we can transcend our ego and its entanglements that lead to our suffering. It is precisely this transcendence of the ego that accompanies us as we live our mundane lives without needing to run away from them. It is also this transcendence that helps us to realize what is popularly known as, "being in the world but not of the world." In essence, we can live a liberated life in spite of our trials and tribulations, and we can still maintain an inward freedom that by and large remains untouched by the external world of our mundane experiences.

It is true that, in daily life situations, equanimity is hard to achieve. The first thing you might say when you get up from reading this book may be, "I'm tired, my back aches," or "I don't like to be in the sun." These thoughts and emotions will start right up after a period of paying close attention.

CHAPTER TWO: STAYING IN THE MOMENT

This chapter will introduce you to the most fundamental and pivotal practice of daily life. All other subsequent practices will be integrated into this primary and basic mindfulness skill. It is the ground or the premise upon which other practices will be added.

From the time we wake up in the morning, we hurry to finish breakfast while we are already thinking of a thousand and one things that we have to do for the coming day. We don't even know what we ate for breakfast. From then on, there is the constant activity of rushing through the day; driving, working, shopping, taking the children to school, cooking, meetings, etc. And amidst this perpetual run-around how do we react to the experiences of the day? We react mostly through the filter of our past memories or through our projections into the future. So we are not fully experiencing the moment because there is either fear of the future or regret about the past impinging on our present moment: so much so that we experience the moment only partially. We are in and out of the moment, with the mind flitting to the past and the future. This way of living in each moment has become our conditioning and has proved to be stressful and exhausting. If not, I dare say that you would not be reading this book.

Thoughts by themselves are not harmful. It is the negative emotions such as anxiety, irritation, fear, and anger, i.e., the negativity that accompanies many of our thoughts, which cause our stress and suffering. If you can stay with your physical sensations there will be no chance for the negative emotions to occupy your mind. Maybe you can stay in the moment for just one nanosecond; but that nanosecond will be enough to derail the string of emotions that dominates the mind. The mind can do only one thing at a time: if it is paying attention to the sensations of the body, the taste of your food, or the ache in your body, it cannot hold fear or anxiety. It will automatically let go. Won't they come back? Yes, they may come back if your mindfulness is not strong enough, and that is why it is important to keep repeating the exercises over and over again. When the practice gets established in your mind, it will give you the skills to break out of habitual slavery to negative emotions and show you a way to live life in a wholesome, engaged manner.

One of my students in our beginner's course was driving to the hospital after her daughter was in a traffic accident. She was very worried about her daughter, and while she was driving to the hospital she began to think, "What if she dies?," or "What if she is maimed," on and on. Then she remembered the Daily Life Mindfulness Practice and decided that she was just going to focus on her driving and stay in the moment. She did that for a little while and suddenly an insight popped up in her mind, "She is not maimed, she is not dead." That simple practice calmed her fears and her anxiety right there and then.

When you're not observing your mind consciously, then what *are* you doing? It is like sleepwalking in a way. If you analyze how your mind works throughout the day, you will invariably find that there are many instances when you react habitually. When you get upset, there may be a lashing out, verbal or otherwise, or else a swirling in the mind. How do we train ourselves to stay in the moment? We do it by learning to pay attention to one of the six senses. Any sensation that you pay attention to in the moment serves as the primary object. The primary object serves as an anchor, which means it anchors the mind in the moment. Invariably your anchor will change from moment to moment as different sights, sounds, smells, and a myriad of things arrive one after another, in succession throughout your day.

You may ask, "How do I deal with so many stimuli throughout the day?" Especially at the outset, you do not need to be aware of everything that you are experiencing. You can choose one sensation out of the five senses to focus on for the day. For example, some people notice touch the most. For others, it may be sound or taste. Whatever grabs your attention the most is the best primary object to use for your daily life practice. For those of you for whom touch is most noticeable, you can pay attention when you are holding a cup or a spoon, touching the keyboard, opening the car door, feeling your fingers on the steering wheel; there are numerous other tactile sensations you can focus on throughout the day. For some, it may be the sensation of taste while drinking and eating; or for others, it may be sound, like water dripping, birds chipping, the hum of the computer, or clocks ticking. Whichever sense is easiest to notice will be the best for keeping focus of throughout the day.

Staying in the moment through noticing physical sensations is the easiest and the most effective way to get out of the habitual rollercoaster state of the mind. It is like putting on the brake to the rollercoaster car. Believe me, applying only one nanosecond of that brake will squelch the momentum. But of course you will need to frequently apply the brakes throughout the day to interrupt the pattern. At first this may not be possible but if you can remember to be mindful just once, you have already begun. The most important thing is to make a firm decision to practice being mindful. A lot of my students will use post-it notes all over their desks, their computers, refrigerators, or dashboards with reminders like BE MINDFUL, BE HERE NOW, STAY IN THE MOMENT, etc. As time goes on, the practice will take hold in your mind and you may not need these reminders any more.

Exercise One: Touch Sensation

This is the most basic exercise of staying with the physical sensation of touch.

You're now touching this book. What do you feel? How do you experience that? You are experiencing the sensation of paper on your hands, aren't you? You can feel the paper, as a bare sensation on the fingers, a very mundane level of sensing an object.

It's the bare experience of the sense of touch in this moment; nothing more, nothing less. It is what is isn't it? This experience is pure, untainted, it just is.

When you go back to reading the book, your attention will shift from holding the book to reading and trying to understand what the book says. When you are reading, your attention is on the book using your sight, and while you are absorbed in the reading you are in the moment. Suppose that while you are reading, the phone rings.

Say you get annoyed because you don't want to stop reading right this minute and go to the phone. But the phone keeps ringing, and you are compelled to get up and take the call. You are talking on the phone, but you are still annoyed because your mind is still on the reading and not on the phone conversation. At that moment, your attention is half-in, half-out. It is split, flitting back and forth between listening and talking to the other person and thinking about your reading. You are not fully present to the caller as your attention goes back and forth between the conversation and your memory of the book. There is annoyance in the back of your mind, and it leaks through into the conversation. Your listening is greatly hampered, you are not completely in the moment of listening and the conversation may become skewed. Even when the conversation has ended and you go back to your reading, you are still carrying the annoyance and so the reading may not be as smooth as you would like. In this scenario, we are seeing how we get attached to the past—even to just a few seconds or a few minutes ago— and how it interferes with the present moment, how it is that we lose track of the moment.

So the practice is to stay as present as possible with each moment. When the phone rings, stay with the sound of the ring completely, and when you get up, leave the reading completely behind. When you walk to the phone, also stay in the moment as you walk to the phone. If you are present in the act of picking up and then listening to the phone, you will have let go of the reading completely and pay full attention to the caller. You will be very present to the other person on the line, and the conversation will be clear and fruitful. When you go back to the reading, if you do the same by being very present, you will not be carrying the memory of the conversation and you can sit down and focus on your reading again without any hang-ups about the conversation and without any annoyance.

Exercise Two: Mindful Eating

Set aside about two minutes and find a few nuts or a piece of fruit or a cookie. Try eating while paying attention through touch, smell, sight, and taste. Just experience whatever is most prominent in the moment in your eating. Your attention may go back and forth between eating and hearing your chewing. Bring your focus back again and again to your primary object, which can be tasted, can be touched, and can be smelled. The primary object helps you to be grounded in the moment. You may have thoughts about the eating, but bring your attention back gently. Don't force yourself, just gently rest in your own experience of eating.

If you don't stay with the experience of eating, your mind will stray and start planning or remembering an unpleasant incident. Then you will lose track of the experience of eating, because your present moment is occupied by thinking of the past or future. Hence you only partially experience the present moment or it may even be taken over by memories and feelings from the past. For example, one of my students who is a financial whiz started this practice and discovered how he had not realized he did not like the foods he was eating because he was always doing something while eating: reading or working on his laptop. When we are mindful we can drop the discursive thinking that brings up memories and emotions and we can experience the moment fully.

Notice this every time you eat, which for most of us takes place two or three times a day, every day. Take a break from your reading right now and get a couple of raisins, nuts, or crackers–whatever you have around that is easy to put your hands on.

Only take two or three pieces. Now go ahead and eat the first small pieces -- a couple of raisins or half a cracker, the way you normally eat. But instead of having your mind wandering all over the place while you eat; to the past or future, whatever; what I would like you to do is focus on any and all of the senses that become predominant while you're eating, as each arises into your awareness. It could be smell, touch, taste, or the muscular movements of your mouth, lips, or jaw. See if you can stay with these different eating sensations, from one to the next, and notice if and when your mind flies about.

Don't close your eyes, this is not the sitting meditation practice. When you're arguing with your boss, you can't say, "Wait a minute, I'm going to go meditate first." You have to respond right away. So in this exercise, keep your eyes open but attend to what is happening right in the moment, and keep your mindfulness focused as carefully as you can.

Suggestions

Some readers may find it easier to stay in the moment when they are showering or walking in the woods, or jogging, driving, biking, cooking, etc. For some it will be sounds and for others it may be tactile sensations. Each person will find the activity or experience that is most prominent and easiest to practice; and at the beginning it is important to stay with the particular activity for at least three weeks.

What To Avoid

The first pitfall that practitioners discover is trying to stay in the moment all day long and then finding themselves tied up in knots. It is practically impossible to be mindful all the time. You will go crazy if you try. There are so many things that we experience and are bombarded by throughout the day; it can wear a person out in the beginning to be mindful of everything and anything. It can also backfire, and you will feel very drained, the practice will seem too difficult and you will feel discouraged. That is why it is important to be selective at first. Work with whatever is easiest and most effective for you, and at the pace that you can manage and be comfortable with.

What you are trying to accomplish is not efficiency of mindfulness at the beginning. You are learning a new *skill*, like skiing, swimming or playing the piano. It's one step at a time. As you become more proficient, your mindfulness will automatically speed up and it will also spread to other activities without even trying.

At first, you may not remember to be in the moment at all, or perhaps only once or twice a day. That is perfectly fine. Rome was not built in a day. Just keep on reminding yourself to be mindful even if you find it difficult. As the days go on, you will realize at certain moments that you have not been mindful: that in itself is being mindful that you have not been mindful. In fact, believe it or not, you have started to be mindful without trying to be mindful. Such is the paradox of the path.

Discussion with Students

Student: First of all, as I was looking at the food – since I was hungry – I noticed the sensation of salivating. Then there was the sensation on my teeth and lips of biting into it. I noticed the saltiness of it. The taste was fairly strong, but trying to stay with it was very difficult.

Dr. T: Yes – but why?

Student: My mind immediately wandered, mostly to sights and thoughts.

Dr. T: But you noticed when it wandered? And did you momentarily go along with the experience of sight, and know that "seeing" was what was happening instead of the eating sensations? And could you go back to the eating?

Student: Yes to all three questions. I caught my attention almost right away, and returned it to the sensations in my mouth.

Dr. T: That's what the practice of staying in the moment is about. You got up to speed in your mindfulness of different sensations dominating, in sequence; which shows that your attention was able to catch up with your experiences while you were eating.

Student: I felt the smoothness of the nuts, and then the pressure of my teeth on them. Then the texture changed from choppy to a smooth kind of mealy feeling, and then flavor came out and it became sweeter and sweeter. Then the sweetness became a sensation that struck my teeth. My mind was not on it all the time.

Dr. T: It does not matter. I just want you to discern through your physical sensations how to stay in the moment and experience the moment with bare attention.

Student: After your introduction to the staying-in-the-moment practice, knowing myself, the best thing for me to do was to find the simplest thing to be mindful of. Each day I made it a point to ground myself in mindfulness for a few moments at a time. I told myself: just stop, don't put in logic or intention, just stop and be mindful here and now. Each day this past week once or twice a day, I would stop and watch myself and say to myself, "Witness it, what is happening in this moment?" I thought that was good enough for me in the first week of practice: simple and easy, but correct.

Dr. T: Were you able to be present then?

Student: Yes, it was easy to be present, but not for very long periods of time.

Dr. T: That's fine: you have already started and that's the most important thing. Your mind cannot by nature stay focused in the moment 24/7. It is literally impossible. Sometimes you will zone out or daydream or forget to practice while you are busy with one thousand and one things. Don't forget, this is just a practice to break the habit of being absorbed in the external all day.

Student: I will often sit in front of the television and mend a garment. What's really happening then. Are those things happening one at a time, or are they happening simultaneously?

Dr. T: One at a time: you are not doing two things simultaneously although it may seem to be the case. You are zoning out to the TV when you attend to your sewing. And when you are watching TV, your mind is not on sewing, even if you are mechanically performing the activity. And you may not really be doing it well, because you are not really focusing on your sewing.

Student: I wonder how I made it so far, doing as much as I do throughout the day without making these choices about managing my attention? It seems like I've been functioning in a trance, could that be true?

Dr. T: No, you made choices before; but it was automatic and through habit. That's the only way you could have made it work. The only difference is now we try to make choices consciously. It's when we don't make clear choices that we get caught up with two or three conflicting needs: that leads to stress. "I want to write, but I need to cook too." "What I really want to do is lie on the couch and rest." Then you become conflicted and unhappy. Part of more easily being able to stay in the moment is making definitive decisions and not looking back. "Ok, I'm going to write and *just* do that. I'm going to cook later." Focus on writing when you are writing and just focus on cooking when you are cooking, so that there is no guilt nibbling at you while you are at these tasks.

There is no rule against multi-tasking. If you can do it well, why not? The only difficulty in multitasking is that emotional reactions may arise, and we carry them around and get stressed out, saying to ourselves, "Oh, I won't be able to finish these three things in one hour, what am I going to do, and I have ten things left for the day." Thus you get caught up in anxiety and fear and all those unpleasant states. Multi-tasking is not stressful in itself; *the stress comes from the added emotion, from mind states, the craving for completion, and then is followed by guilt, self judgment, and so on.* This is an American phenomenon. You have twenty things on your list; you've got to finish all of them. If not, you're not up to the mark. This is a very achievement-oriented society. I don't recall ever writing to-do lists when I lived in Burma but here in U.S. I have become like everybody else; each day I make a to-do list.

Student: Do you agonize about your list?

Dr. T: Oh, no. I do what I can and if I don't have time I leave them for the next day or some other time, unless there is a deadline. Then I will tackle that task and then leave the rest for later on. I use the list just as a reminder, not a commandment! That's probably the difference. We need to rule the list, not let the list rule us!

Beth: I thought about the kind of things I could do to remind myself to practice. So I took my shower every morning as a way to ground myself and quiet down. I paid attention to each moment of my bodily movements and to all the sensations: sounds, smells, and so on. And then throughout the day, I chose to try to listen to sounds, because I found that really effective. It would only last a few seconds before a thought would come up, and then I would say, "Oh, look at that, I'm thinking about something," and I'd bring my attention back to sounds.

Dr. T: You each will naturally be able to choose whatever is the most suitable for you to be mindful of. For some people it's eating, for some it's walking, for some it's driving. Once you choose, you'll automatically screen out what you're not choosing to be mindful of; and no two people will choose the same for this practice, and that's okay.

Nettie: I did a task each day to practice mindfulness. And I do feel that towards the end of the week, there was an accumulation, a more frequent remembering to pay attention to what I was doing, and I was also more frequently aware of when I would get sidetracked and daydream. And I almost felt like the sidetracking didn't last as long and I seemed to develop a habit. Also, you said last week to be mindful of whatever was the dominant sense object in the moment. So I worked a little with that: I was walking and I focused on whatever presented itself; a smell, a daydream, a thought, a worry, or the feeling of my feet walking. It was so interesting because, when I got to the end of it, it's like I was just a mosaic of all these little things.

Dr. T: You see, that's the whole trick. When you turn your attention to a new object, you practice leaving the past behind. The moment you leave task number one, that task is the past, it's gone; now grab onto the present task, with a mind empty of the first task, empty of reactions about it. When that is done, go back to the first or on to the next, and leave the second behind. You are learning how to not carry the past with you, even the past of just a few seconds before. Let go of the past, move to what is present, and then be totally present. If you carry the past of one second before, then that becomes the new problem!

Joanne: I'm in the middle of renovating a new house, so there's chaos everywhere. I had left work to wait for someone to come and help me, and the person didn't show up. I was very—shall we say—mindful of my emotions, I had so much to do and felt the stress building. I was present with the fact that I was irritated, there was nothing I could do about it: it was a habitual reaction to this person's chronic lateness. I analyzed what was going on, and made a conscious choice to arrange some flowers. I had many, many things to do, and so I chose one of the projects that needed to be done, and dissipated the reaction that way, by focusing carefully on what I was doing. And once I finished that project, I said to myself —be present, just go back to the office and do your work there. So I went through a sequence: mindfulness of the reaction plus analyzing the reaction plus not overreacting plus making a choice. It worked out pretty well.

Betty: While doing the eating practice, I found myself going off to thoughts of, "Oh, I really don't like these nuts." But when I went back to the eating sensations, I noticed that my thoughts stopped, at least momentarily.

Dr. T: Especially when the eyes are open, as we do in daily life practice, your attention will go back and forth between sight and mouth sensations, as well as other objects. You can see by doing this exercise that the mind is very fast. In Buddhist psychology, it is said that with a flicker of an eyelid, **billions** of thought-moments have passed. If you don't practice returning your attention to the experience of eating, you will find that your mind is always churning up thoughts like, "Oh, I don't like peanuts, why did I pick peanuts? That was dumb of me." This is how your mind creates all its habits of negativity and defilement like ill-will towards peanuts and toward yourself too! You can see very clearly how greed and ill-will arise through the five senses in the simple exercise of paying attention during eating. But when Betty started to chew and concentrated on just the experience of eating, then that ill-will began to fall away, because nothing stays in the mind, everything is impermanent. So she can go back to just experiencing the peanuts without ill-will.

Student: I think this would be a very good for dieting, because I noticed that when I really ate with mindfulness, it was more satisfying. I got into each taste in each mouthful of food.

Dr. T: That's what a lot of people say about the eating practice. We tend to gulp food unconsciously; we're either reading or talking to each other or on the phone. Even if we're all alone, we don't concentrate on eating, our thoughts are running away; imagining what's going to happen, planning for the next day, thinking about the past, or thinking, "I could have cooked a better meal." There's a running commentary in the mind, and you're not really experiencing the food. That's one way we become addicted to food, the experience of eating is not satisfactory, so we want a better kind of food, tastier food, more food. We try to cook gorgeous meals; we cook five kinds of dishes in a meal. But if you really focus on the food you're eating, it may not be something that you like, but if you really pay attention to what you're experiencing in the eating, you'll find that food in itself is pleasant, or at worst, neutral. But for right now, just practice staying in the moment and experiencing the five physical senses while eating; do this practice at least once a day with one meal for two weeks. I think that you'll be very surprised by what you discover.

These first daily life practices help you learn how to stay with the stimulus that is impacting on your senses, at the moment of contact – now! Ultimately, the goal of this practice is to be able to stay with the impact of each object so that the mind is completely at rest in the face of the impact. that is equanimity. We will develop our own inner buffer zone, the inner silence that was discussed earlier, because we don't have the luxury of outer silence. Every day, we are exposed to everything -- beautiful things, wonderful things, difficult things, very different kinds of events and people, and the natural elements too; rain, heat, everything that life throws at us. But even a momentary silence is enough to keep you grounded. You will all naturally be able to choose whatever is the most suitable for you to be mindful of. For some people it's eating, for some it's walking, for some it's driving. Once you choose, you'll automatically screen out what you're not choosing to be mindful of; and you will find out what works best for you and you can use that as your practice theme. Try practicing for two weeks. I think that you'll be very surprised by what you discover.

Exercise Three: Listening and Speaking

When you're conversing, try to stay very present to the person you're talking to. When you are talking, are you really present with that person or is there a running commentary in your mind? When you're speaking, you might be thinking, "I'd rather be somewhere else than talking to this person." The practice is to stay there with the person, for the person, and to be very present right in the moment.

The practice is to be with the other, not just to be with yourself. Often, we want to take over the conversation, we want to interject; we want to prove our points, give our opinions, cut the other person down when we're irritated. So, even when the person is very difficult, the practice is to be there, to stay with the difficulty. See what is happening with the other person and with yourself. That is the practice.

Discussion with Students

Student: After you assigned this exercise I tried to be mindful in conversation with people, and I found that I had quite a few flashes of reaction that went through my mind as I was listening to what a person was saying; usually assumptions or prejudicial remarks. They went by so fast I couldn't have even said the word describing the reaction that quickly. But it was interesting to see that. When I could do it, it worked, but it was very hard to do it for very long.

Student: I had a situation like the cooking/telephone scenario happen last week. I was listening to a very interesting political discussion on the radio and the phone rang. I left the radio and it was a friend who had just gotten back from a long trip, so of course they wanted to tell me about the trip. I had to tune out the radio completely in order to listen. I did OK, but at first I was irritated. And if I was really being present, I would have asked them to excuse me for a moment so I could turn off my radio. I wasn't that present, but I was able to tune out the radio and focus on listening.

Student: What exactly is mindfulness in the moment?

Dr. T: The mental faculty of mindfulness is like a doorman standing in front of a hotel door and paying attention to whoever is coming in and going out. In terms of this first practice, you're minding your sense doors, what sensations are coming in and going out, what senses are being stimulated one after the other. In one of the scriptures, the Buddha gave an example of a hunter. If you were hunting a deer, you hide behind a bush and are very quiet. You would be very aware of all of the animals in the vicinity. Exactly this way, the mind that is trying to catch the mind has to be very quiet, as still as a hunter who is waiting for animals to be seen. In this way, you can catch your thoughts, your sensations, and your emotions by waiting in silence.

Student: Why is the mind called the sixth sense? I thought that meant something about intuition.

Dr. T: In Buddhist psychology, the sixth sense *is* the mind, or what is called the mind-door, not the intuitive sense. It is considered to be a sense door that lets objects into awareness, just like the other physical senses. Its objects are any mind states: thoughts, emotions, memories, projections, perceptions, fantasies, planning, ideas, ideals, anything that happens in the mind is called a mind object. If you're meditating, like just now when you were trying the eating practice, some of you were probably very aware that your thoughts were running away, and hopefully you could catch them at some point. In catching the mind at that moment, what you notice becomes the new object of your meditation.

Student: Would you say spiritual practice is a matter of changing the mind?

Dr. T: No, it's about changing the *habits* of the mind, the conditioned habits of the mind, which usually bring us suffering. Do they not? We are conditioned to ruminate about the past, be fearful of the future and create our own dramas around incidents, people, and events. Meditation is intended to break this kind of habit. When the habits change, your mind will change automatically.

Student: I might be getting ahead of the game, but when we're talking about the mind catching itself, for instance getting angry... Okay, I catch it, now what should I do?

Dr. T: Just stay with the anger and then do nothing, let it be. Meaning, let it be held gently with your mindfulness. If you try to control anger, you're on the wrong track. If you repress it, hold it inside, what happens? It'll blow up later, or escape in other detrimental ways. No, the idea is to notice it and let it take its own course. No thought or feeling will last unless you actively hang on to it, feed it, act on it, or you dwell on it. No single emotion or thought will stay unless you cling to it and nurture it and build on it. By clinging, you prolong your emotions and other painful mind states. By clinging to past events that made you angry, clinging to ideas of the person who hurt you, clinging to events, situations, experiences, things, possession, to *anything*, suffering is prolonged. If you learn to catch and then to stay with your mind states, they will die down in their own time; just don't interfere with the process. But you're right; you are getting ahead of yourself!

For now, for the next two weeks, focus on doing the three practices outlined in this chapter. Then move on to the next chapter, and after that, you'll be working on the more advanced practices, which will address just what you're asking about.

CHAPTER THREE:
MINDFULNESS OF PEACE MIND

The second practice we will look at is, Mindfulness of Peaceful Mind States. This is a transitional practice, where you will move from paying attention to the five physical senses to paying attention more fully to your mind itself using the same principle of staying in the moment. At this stage, your focus of staying in the moment is not on your physical sensations but on the peaceful nature of your mind itself.

How do we do this? Now, right this moment, while you are reading this book, on this line, and on this page, are you angry? Are you stressed out? Are you fearful? Are you in mental pain? I am quite sure you are not; otherwise you would not be able to focus on the words on this page.

So let's say you are fairly quiet in your mind. You may be curious about what I am going to write next, but, in general, you are quiet and at peace, right? My question to you is this, "What did you have to do to be at peace at this very moment?" You might say, "I am focused on reading your book, so I am not in conflict with anyone or with anything. As a result, I am relatively at peace." I would agree. However, you might think this sense of peace can be disrupted at any time. For example, if someone comes in and starts yelling or the doorbell rings, it would disturb your peace. But our situation is still hypothetical and those things haven't happened yet. What I would like you to consider, right this minute is; are you at peace? At this very instant, right now, can you experience the peace in your mind? If so, you have already started on your second practice; *to experience the peaceful mind states in your mind.*

Maybe you will say, "But this peace is not going to last." That's perfectly true. It may not last. When does it end? Isn't it when you start to think about something that has bothered you in the past or maybe something might begin to bother you right this minute, like the telephone ringing or someone wanting to talk to you? Then perhaps you get annoyed and the peacefulness you were experiencing is gone! But what if I were to suggest that you use the first practice of staying in the moment to talk to whoever is talking to you. While you are conversing, you will not be able to feel peace because you will be busy listening and talking. If the person should annoy you, you may feel you have completely lost your peace of mind. If that happens, just stay with the moment of annoyance and let it be. The annoyance will not stay too long if you let it be. Once it is gone, you will be back to your peaceful state.

We are not talking about permanent peace, we are just exploring whether there is such a thing as peaceful nature in our own mind. If you agree with me that there is, then I would love to discuss further about it. Granted, this peaceful state is not permanent but my question again is, "When do you lose it?" You might say, "When someone makes me angry," or "when I am in terrible traffic," or "When I am in the throes of meeting a deadline." Sure, in those examples you would have lost the peaceful feeling and would have become overwhelmed by all kinds of emotions. But doesn't anger always end, don't you get over traffic jams, and don't deadlines pass? When those things are all over, what happens then? You feel a great relief, don't you? And you are also at ease. Now then, this is what I call the peaceful nature of mind, i.e., the ease of being, just that. Isn't that sense of ease the same as what you are feeling now? Feeling fine, just as you are, without having to try to be peaceful?

Right now are you meditating? Are you not fairly peaceful in this moment? The peacefulness you are feeling right this minute "just is," isn't it? Its just a natural place in the mind when there is no strife, where there is a natural peace. What I want to emphasize is that this peaceful state is part of the nature of our mind; just as anger, sadness, jealousy, joy, and compassion are all part of the whole repertoire of our own mind.

Why are we so hung-up on the idea that we have no peace of mind? Why do we run around trying to find it at meditation centers, with gurus, with all kinds of Dhamma* teachers? It's because we remember only the suffering when we experience anger, sadness, etc.

Exercise One: Fingers and Space

Now I am going to do a little exercise, which I call my Burmese koan. If you spread out your five fingers and look at your hand. What do you see? The five fingers, no doubt, as well as the back of the hand or the palm, the wrist, or the lines on the palms. You will notice the solid structure of your hands first. What about the space in between the fingers? I am sure that now that I have mentioned it, you will take notice of that space and say, "Oh yes, there is space in between the fingers." Now why is it we only notice the solid structures of the hands and not the space? *It's because it's more obvious isn't it?* In other words, we miss out on what is not obvious–the space between the fingers. This is a metaphor of our life. We tend to remember only the times we are upset, when we are suffering, because they are more obvious and we can hold them in our memory bank. We tend to overlook the intervals when we are not upset or sad or suffering; when we are actually mostly peaceful and feeling fine. We tend to lose track of these peaceful intervals and noticing how they help us to rest in ourselves after all our emotional upheaval and turmoil. Without these relatively peaceful moments we would all be in the mad house, including the author.

You cannot be angry twenty-four-hours a day, you cannot be jealous for that length either. Even during extremely difficult times we still need to cook, eat, and drink. In other words we need to take time out from our suffering. It is during these unconscious or conscious time-outs that we take a break from suffering. It is during these intervals that we rest our mind or relax and rejuvenate ourselves, but usually without ever noticing the natural way our minds regulates itself. There is a limit to which our minds can hold a very difficult emotion such as anger, sadness, or mental pain. We will invariably try to find a way to ease it, like talking to a friend or a therapist, going to a movie, taking a walk, or whatever helps. These periods allow the mind to rest and take a break from its perpetual motion.

Now suppose we make it a point to notice these intervals of less suffering or relative peace and focus on how we feel? Wouldn't that serve us better, instead of focusing on things that make us angry, sad or fearful? The practice now is to rest in this peaceful state of mind and try to experience it throughout the day. If you can do it only once or twice a day that's perfectly fine. What I would like you to realize is that it is part of the nature of your own mind. You do not have to run around trying to find it. *It is right there with you, in you.* It has been there since you were born and it will be there until the day you die. It will not leave you unless you choose to ignore it or to overlook it. In other words, I am advocating that you can use the peaceful nature of your mind as a primary object, or focus, for your mindfulness practice. Just like the breath is used to practice sitting meditation, you can use the peaceful nature of your own mind as your meditation practice. And you don't even have to carry your meditation cushion around. Because the peaceful nature is there within your mind and unlike a meditation cushion it goes everywhere with you! It's there in crowds or traffic, at work, home, or at meetings; anywhere and everywhere.

Exercise Two: What Was There Before the Bell?

Let's try a second exercise. Ring a bell if you have one. If not, just use a glass and strike a spoon against it. You will only strike it once. Now after striking the bell or the glass, just listen until the sound dies away. Now, my question for you is, "What was there before the sound?"

Contemplate on it for a while. Was there a sound before you struck the bell or the glass? There was only silence, wasn't there?

Likewise, in your daily life, before anything hits your mind to make you angry, sad or worry; is there, in your mind, already any anger, sadness or worry? No. Your mind just *was*. There was neither happiness nor unhappiness. Let's look at what that *just was* is like. Were you quite comfortable in yourself before the anger, sadness or worry arose, just like it is now, while you are reading this book? It is that level of ease and comfort that I am talking about. We can always come back to it when we are aware that we have this natural sense of ease and peace in us. No need to run around trying to find it elsewhere outside of ourselves; its like coming home to rest, after all the stress and difficult emotional states have worn us out.

It's one of the most precious things we have in us and it is free too, for that matter! Nothing can beat it.

Discussion with Students

Student: I try to watch my peace mind, but the peace only lasts for a flicker of a second and then I am already on to thinking or feeling something or I am distracted by things in my environment.

Dr. T: That flicker is most crucial because you have already started experiencing the peaceful nature of your mind. It's a break in a long series of thinking, emoting, and doing. It shows that you can experience the peaceful nature of your mind in spite of being busy; doing and feeling, etc.

Student: When it was described how to be with my peace mind it almost sounded like any thinking needs to be avoided.

Dr. T: In the moment of experiencing the peace there will be no thought. If there is thinking, you will not be able to experience the peace explicitly. So you don't have to worry about avoiding thinking or not avoiding thinking. The moments of thinking will automatically come back right after the moment of peace has passed. It is a natural process. We can experience the peaceful nature of our mind only when our discursive thinking stops. When I say that, people immediately ask, "Don't we need to think about what we're doing tomorrow?" or "Don't we need to think about what we're making for dinner?"

Planning is fine; as is assessing, analyzing, remembering, and all the other ordinary functions of the mind. But when you intentionally practice looking at your peaceful states, the practice is to stop the discursive mind and to just experience the peaceful nature of the mind. This practice is just like trying to stay in the moment with the physical sensations of taste, touch, etc. The moment you feed your thoughts, they take you away from experiencing the innate nature of your mind.

Student: Suppose anger arises through inner or outer contact. Should we let our reaction have a natural life of its own, then let it slowly dissipate, as happens in our ordinary minds? Then, after the storm, would we go into the space between, into the peace? Do we permit an expression of that angry reaction to occur, or do we perhaps intellectualize it, "Don't be upset, it wasn't a car accident," and keep it somehow inside ourselves?

Dr. T: Thank you for bringing that up. Let me answer the first part of your question. Yes, we let our reactions dissipate by themselves. The important thing is to not start ruminating about that anger. Instead, just let it be and keep watching it like a witness until it fades away. When it fades away, you will be automatically in the peaceful state without even trying.

As for the latter part of your question; yes, if you can rationalize the situation in order to temper the unwholesome reaction, it's well and good. But it depends on how you think about it. If you rationalize in angry or negative terms, you're off. For example, if you think, "What a bummer, look at the kinds of people that are on the road. Things are just getting worse on the highways."

Student: So focus on the positive, "I wasn't in an accident."

Dr. T: Right. Then you'll be fine. That helps stabilize the mind. But you also have to let the anger be as it is, and not act on it. But you have to be very careful. That's why, in the beginning, I don't ask students to look directly into the anger. If you habitually and positively rationalize, that's fine for now. But if you are habitually acting through your anger, or thinking through your anger, then be careful: you will add fuel to your anger. So be careful when you rationalize; you need to rationalize without anger. If you can, that's okay. But if you cannot, then do the exercises from the first chapter, maybe go back to focusing on the breath or to the sensation of your hands on the steering wheel. It may save lives!

Student: It still sounds like any thinking needs to be avoided.

Dr. T: We need to delineate between functional thinking and thinking that has a lot of emotional overlay. We need to think and plan for the next day, where to go, what to do etc. These are functional thoughts and are absolutely necessary so that we face fewer problems as we go through the day. What I mean by "not thinking," is only for the practice of being mindful of our emotional states. That's when we need to stop thinking and just simply watch our emotions which in Buddhism we talk about as "bare attention." You watch your emotions like you would watch your breath, without engaging in discursive thinking.

Student: So when you say "think," what you mean is a lot of thought, automatic thoughts.

Dr. T: Automatic thoughts and also automatic emotional reactions. It depends too on how those automatic thoughts are taking place and what they are. Are they wholesome thoughts or unwholesome, negative thoughts? Are they thoughts of anger? Are they thoughts colored with dissatisfaction, ill-will, or greed?

Student: So when being mindful and intentionally practicing looking at your peaceful states, the rule is, no additional thinking.

Dr. T: Absolutely. The moment you bring up a thought, it takes you away from the main events transpiring in your mind. For example, if you're practicing watching your peaceful state, the moment you entertain a thought, the peaceful state is already gone. You lose the moment of peace. The practice boils down to that.

When your mind is at least momentarily clear of emotional negative states, then you'll be able to see any little doubts, thoughts, moving in. Whereas, if the mind is already jumbled and full; you won't be able to detect any thoughts that are popping up. When you're at peace, that's when you want to really focus on your practice. When you are new to the practice and find that your mind is chaotic, go for a walk, get some ice cream, or talk to a friend until your mind settles down. When your mind is quiet, then focus gently on that peaceful state. We want to see how many times during the day you can check in and see that you're at peace. Keep a journal, if that's helpful. If it's only twice, write those instances down. One time or no time, that's fine. In the beginning, you want to see how much you are perhaps already aware of peaceful moments.

Say, for example, that your mind becomes peaceful. When you're at peace and you're staying with the peaceful state, you'll find that if there's even a little wavering of the mind, you notice it very clearly. You see how it wavers and then if you don't get upset about it, it tapers off and you're back to the peaceful state. Or, conversely, you'll see how the entrance of a thought will, if you feed it, causes the peaceful state to taper off, and you're back to thinking all the time! Generally, when you are new to a practice, you'll mostly see the ending of thoughts and emotions. Your mindfulness hasn't moved quickly enough to see the arising of these mind states. Suddenly you'll realize, "Oops, I've been thinking for the last five minutes." But that's fine. In that moment, in fact, you're already being mindful that you were not mindful. So it's a good beginning.

Student: What about states that are relatively neutral or the "nothing" kind of busyness that goes on in the mind a lot of the time. It's neither positive nor negative, it's just busy thoughts. Is that a mind at peace? It's not anger, it's not fear, it's not bliss; it's just stuff going on.

Dr. T: It depends on how you experience that state. You can be very busy in your mind and yet not feel stressed. But this depends on how clean your thoughts are, i.e., without attendant negative emotions.

Student: It's very difficult.

Dr. T: Why do you think so?

Student: Because I'm usually planning ahead. So I'm not really present in the moment.

Dr. T: When you plan ahead, how do you plan?

Student: I try to be prepared.

Dr. T: "Try." Let's look at that word. Investigation is a very important part of Buddhist practice. In fact its one of the mental factors you'll be reading about later in this book. But, for now, is this trying due to desire?

Student: Yes.

Dr. T: Okay, desire for what?

Student: To do the best.

Dr. T: Desire for the best. What is "best?"

Student: The ideal you have of what you want in life.

Dr. T: Yes, it's an ideal. An ideal, is that real?

Student: I believe it's real.

Dr. T: Believing is not reality is it? It's definitely a concept. It's not a real event or outcome. So you are trying for your desire, you have a goal, and you try to get to the goal. This implies that you may also have thoughts about not accomplishing it.

Student: Fear.

Dr. T: Yes, there you are. Goals and ideals are fine: but they can, if we let them, generate fear. Fear, in Buddhism, is a category of ill-will. It is ill-will towards the future. Fear can be based on our mind contacting memories of the past and projecting them into the future, and that's what often makes planning stressful. Planning by itself is okay: if we don't plan, we won't accomplish anything. You usually can't live just floating from day to day; you need to do some strategizing and planning. But it depends on how we plan, and if that planning generates fear and worry and other unwholesome states. Anxiety, worry, they're all ill-will towards the future. Can you just do "pure planning?" That would be a good practice for you; simple, pure planning.

Student: I can conceptualize "pure planning." However, if a plan falls through, then I drop into chaos and worry.

Dr. T: Again, what you will be able to do—if the practice is done correctly—is accept the fact that the plan fell through and be okay with it. It's especially important, if you have a lot of worry or stress, to remember that you do have these episodes of peace, these intervals of peaceful states, and that they will always be there. You need only remember to go to them.

CHAPTER FOUR:
THE CYCLE OF CONDITIONING

Now we are getting into the core practices of DLMP meditation which are the basis of developing equanimity. There are three practices which will build up the quality of equanimity in us:

1. Mindfulness of likes and dislikes

2. Mindfulness of value judgments

3. Mindfulness of clinging

Before getting into the nitty-gritty of these practices, let me first describe how our mind works in everyday situations when we are challenged by the onslaught of our environment; be it family life, work life, social or political life, or even our own mind. I have presented this in the form of a diagram which my students use as their working model to understand how we end up suffering. They also use the diagram as the visual aid for their practice and it has been the key to the success of their mindfulness meditation. I call this diagram the Cycle of Conditioning or Suffering.

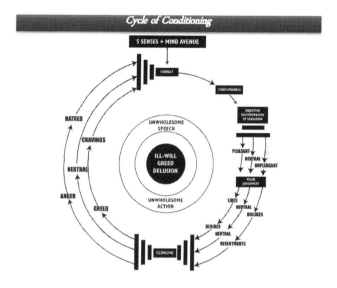

Diagram 4.1: The Cycle of Conditioning

Contact

If you look at the diagram you will see that the top of the page presents the contact point between our six senses and external stimuli. The impact of this contact sets up a wave of rapid, successive responses in our mind. This diagram is an expansion of this spark into the fully blown Cycle of Conditioning depicting the process of what happens in the mind after contact.

Consciousness

The first reaction in the cycle is pure consciousness through the five senses which in Buddhism is described as "seeing consciousness," i.e., you can see words on this page; "hearing consciousness," i.e., if you should hear some sounds; "touch consciousness," i.e., your hand touching this book, etc. At this stage it is pure seeing, pure hearing, etc.

A good example of pure consciousness might be the feeling upon first awakening in the morning and thinking they didn't know where they were. But very soon they realize, "Oh yes, I'm in my own bed." Their initial reaction to that first hit of contact through their eyes is pure consciousness, because it does not yet contain any discrimination.

Sense Perception and Discrimination

The second reaction moment, which depicts the second link on the cycle, contains cognition through sensory input. Now the mind starts to differentiate between different types of sensations. In terms of mindfulness practice, discrimination is classified only in the broad terms of pleasant, unpleasant or neutral. These sensations can be very strong, soft or unbearable. But the sensations are impermanent and changeable. Our reaction to sensations is also changeable. For example, when I was growing up in Burma, I used to dislike cilantro because I disliked its strong aroma. But later on, after living in Thailand for nine years, I grew to be fond of cilantro because every single Thai dish is garnished with cilantro and it was impossible to avoid it. Now I am hooked on it and will pinch and smell it before I buy it to make sure it has that strong aroma. Cilantro to me has changed from being unpleasant to pleasant.

Both pleasant and unpleasant can change to neutral too. If my nose were stuffed up it would not matter whether the cilantro is aromatic or not. We can see that all our mental reactions are conditional. When you are sick, the same food may taste differently. Even the most scrumptious meal may seem repelling.

Value Judgments

From sensations we move on very quickly to value judgments. Like sensations, value judgments are also positive, negative or neutral. They can also move back and forth. All three states are impermanent and conditional. For example, two people fall in love and get married. Five years later they can't stand each other anymore and split. After twenty years both people are old and decrepit and, when they meet again, are just friends.

Don't we think the person we married is perfect and will never change? That is what is called delusion in Buddhism; the delusion that things will always be permanent and unchangeable. Again the impermanence of value judgments is also conditional on our internal and external circumstances.

Likes and Dislikes

The next reaction that follows value judgments will depend on whether they are positive, negative or neutral. Positive value judgments will be followed by liking in our minds and negative value judgments will be followed by disliking. Neutral occurs when you don't make any judgments.

Now liking and disliking can intensify into desire or resentment. Desire may intensify into craving then into grasping (clinging) and even obsession. Resentment turns into anger which, in turn, can lead to hatred. By nature they are the same kind of emotion, i.e. ill-will with the intensity of the emotion as the main variable for each.

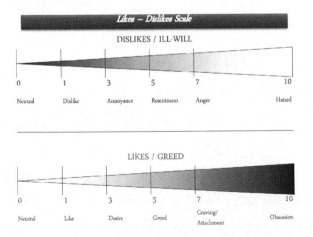

Diagram 4.2: Likes/Dislikes Scale

I have used the above scale of 0-10 to demonstrate the variation in the intensities of common feelings to give you a sense of how they are related and how they may still be present at different intensities if we are not conscious of our own mind.

These likes and dislikes tend to translate into speech and behavior. In the flicker of an eyelid billions of cycles pass and that's how conditioning ensues. Once we end up in this kind of cycle we tend to own it and it becomes our behavior pattern for a long time until we chose to break this mental pattern.

Clinging

Clinging happens when desire/craving intensifies and it can happen to anything.

In Buddhism there are three areas that clinging happens:

1. Everything in this sense world; be it people, animals, inanimate objects, ideas, doctrines, power, fame, etc.

2. Existence, life itself, and fear of death

3. Non-existence; rejecting one's life, e.g., suicidal tendencies

When there is clinging, emotional states build up to a large extent and to an extreme that can lead to obsessions and addictions which are very difficult to alleviate and require a very strong mindfulness practice to do so.

We see the links on the left-hand side of the cycle depicting very strong emotions, such as greed, anger, and hatred, which cause intense suffering in us. In the untrained mind, they spill over to unwholesome speech and unwholesome action. These are very prone to habit forming and as such we find our behavior becoming very ingrained and difficult to change for the better.

Then the question is, how do you practice DLMP in this kind of mental and emotional merry-go-round? Out of the three core practices, likes and dislikes are the easiest to detect and use as your object of mindfulness; even though they arise after value judgments. So we choose to practice on likes and dislikes first out of the three. Mindfulness on judgments is more challenging, so it is used as the second practice.

We use clinging as the last practice because it is very subtle and requires greater skill to being mindful. The idea is by being mindful of one of these states you can exit the cycle at that particular link so that your emotions don't run away from you to the hard-core emotions like anger, hatred or grasping and obsession. But as your practice matures you will be able to handle those more intense reactions too.

CHAPTER FIVE:
MINDFULNESS ON LIKES AND DISLIKES

EXERCISE ONE

We have touched on the general idea of the core practices through the Cycle of Conditioning and now we will go into more specific ways of how to practice them. Let's start with mindfulness on likes and dislikes.

Look around your room or the place where you are now, and find something that bothers you; a sight, sound, person, smell, whatever it may be. Focus your attention on the object, then immediately turn your attention away from the object and look directly at the feeling of dislike in your mind. If you see the feeling of dislike in your mind just keep on watching it like you watch your breath, without discursive thoughts. As you keep watching you will find the feeling of dislike will start to diminish and then fade away. If you cannot discern the feeling try again by looking at a more disturbing scene and then turn towards your feeling and repeat the same.

This practice is simple mechanics, nothing mystical. You are just replacing your feeling of dislike with the mental act of watching it. When you turn inwards and watch it the dislike will be gone and you will be just left with watching. The important thing is to not engage with the dislike in any way; it is a matter of letting it be. All thoughts and feelings have their own lifespan and will die their own natural death—unless we cling to them. Do the same with the feeling of liking. You can try eating something delicious, ice cream, for example. Eat it as usual. When the ice cream is in your mouth you will feel the cool, delicious flavor and texture and your enjoyment of it. Keep tabs on your sense pleasure. As soon as the ice cream passes and disappears from your tongue do you still feel the pleasurable feeling of the aftertaste? Now keep on watching the aftertaste and look into your mind. You will invariably find your feeling of liking it and wanting more of it. Just watch your liking and you will see that it will diminish and then disappear.

Sometimes your discursive thoughts may arise while you are watching your feeling. That is fine, just gently go back to the feeling of liking and try staying there as much as possible. The purpose of this exercise is to demonstrate how we can watch our likes and dislikes before they manifest into desire, craving and grasping. When we cannot stop at liking but go on to craving and grasping for certain foods, don't we sometimes go out of the way to get it no matter what? Coffee would be one good example. If you drink it, maybe coffee would be a good thing for you to practice on. It may help those who are dependent on it to reduce their intake.

Discussion with Students

Student: I was able to watch small things that I dislike. For example, at my gym someone got on the machine right next to me when there were a lot of other machines in the room. I felt my space was being impinged upon and I disliked it. It was minor so it did not bother me too much and I was able to watch it and let it be. After a while it was gone and I could concentrate on my own exercise. I am also starting to notice other things that I dislike when the feeling stayed longer. In these moments, I have not been able to come to that place of just observing the dislike, but instead get caught in it for some time. So it's been 50/50 this past week.

Dr. T: The practice is just to be more aware of your own mental processes. It's not a competition. We just want to see how we get caught up in the consequences of likes and dislikes. It does not mean we have to abolish all dislikes and just keep your likes. Even the dislikes that continue to generate some suffering where are they right now?

Are there still here right now in your mind?

Student: No.

Dr. T: Those dislike are only memories now aren't they? They were there before but now they're gone.

Student: I looked at that lamp in the room here and immediately felt a dislike. When I focused on how I was feeling, memories came up about an incident recently when I broke a lamp exactly like this one. So every time I look at this lamp, that memory comes up. So I'm not sure if I dislike the lamp in this room or my memory of the broken lamp.

Dr. T: The lamp here serves as a trigger. Your memory of breaking the other lamp was the actual cause of your dislike. That old memory was inserting itself when you first looked at this lamp. So the present moment was overpowered by the memory of the past and influenced your reaction to this present lamp. But what is important is that you experienced an insight right away that it was your memory that caused the dislike. This is what we mean by *experiential insight* within Insight Meditation or a mindfulness practice. These insights come from our own innate intelligence, which is in all of us, there are no exceptions! First, you mistakenly thought it was this lamp that was bothering you. But at the moment that you recognized it was your memory of the past that was responsible for your feelings, your delusion dropped and insight arose simultaneously and instantaneously.

I have been asked many times how insight arises in DLMP. This is an example of how experiential insight arises right at the moment of experiencing a mundane incident. The insight that occurs from the incident is of the spiritual kind because it enables the individual to break out of their delusion (she was able to transcend the delusion that she disliked the lamp in the room but the moment that she transcended her delusion she saw the actual truth in the moment that it was her clinging to the memory of the past.) This seeing is what is called insight or panna* in Buddhist scriptural language.

The example here is dealing with a relatively easy state of annoyance; it was easy for her to go through the process, to have insight into that particular filter. Going through this process many times, practicing with relatively easy objects of like and dislike, will build up your power of concentration and your confidence, since you're not tackling the big areas of delusion or suffering in your life. The concentration you bring to looking into your mind is the same kind of concentration you bring when you are practicing sitting meditation. Your mind is collected and stays with one point, one experience, it isn't scattered. It is also this way in The Daily

Life Mindfulness Practice, although your concentration will not be as deep as it can be during sitting meditation, there is still some level of concentration, of one-pointedness. It takes a lot of mental energy to be able to turn inwards and stay with one's own mind especially with a negative mind state. I think it's even harder than concentrating on your breath. It's also deeper because you're not just observing your mind; you're also comprehending what is happening there. That's what mindfulness means: not just seeing, but also knowing and investigating what is.

The result is that you can exit the cycle of conditioning. And when you exit the cycle, then you are reconditioning yourself. You are transforming your inner state.

Student: I dislike a Styrofoam cup that I'm seeing right now, but it's not the cup, it's more the idea of disposability behind the cup.

Dr. T: We have all kinds of examples to show us how we get stuck in our conditioning, our filters. Earlier we were looking at a real object that bothered one of you, then a memory, now we are looking at the conditioning of concepts. Here again it is the association that comes with the object and not just the object itself. Isn't it how we choose even religious and political doctrines? It is all based on our likes and dislikes according to how we are conditioned by our past or present experiences.

Student: Last week I was able to practice watching liking and disliking because I was really sick. I practiced on my dislike of what I was feeling physically. So I tried to stay with the feelings as much as possible and I went back to the first practice of staying in the moment, and used simple physical contacts with my environment as anchors to stay present. I was sitting on my couch all afternoon just doing that, staying with sensations as much as I could, and I wasn't judging it too much, or clinging to what I thought it should be like. I kept seeing some clinging arise, and I simply said, "Okay, bye." I got closer and closer with my attention to the "sick" sensations, and it was a strange, bizarre feeling of getting right there with the feelings as they were happening. It was without my usual judgment, so the physical discomfort wasn't really there in the end. After a while, I wasn't experiencing it as a negative thing. I stopped feeling so bad. In fact, I started to feel good, so the literal sensations of the discomfort just stopped.

Dr. T: You were experiencing only the process of it, the pure nature of the physical sensations without added filters of "this is pleasant, this is unpleasant, I like this, I don't like this." You peeled off layers and layers of filters, right down to the very pure sensation. You got to the point of seeing physical phenomenon of your body as it happens in its *suchness*. This is also another of those "experiential insights" that happen when the mind is concentrated and in equilibrium with mindfulness and all thoughts and emotions fall away.

Student: I find that when I'm conversing with people, I want to interject something about myself, something that makes me look smarter and give a boost to my self-image. I notice that I get that urge, but I don't follow the urge when I notice it. And since I've stopped doing that, I notice that I feel more connected with people! I think there is a craving for recognition and the clinging to wanting to shape people's opinions of me. I feel like I've been able to be mindful of that coming up and just see it and follow it. I'm able to be mindful of my craving but not act on it.

Dr. T: Yes, by the fact that you intentionally stopped acting with your usual pattern you are already freed of the Cycle of Suffering. And you also found the result is more pleasant and beneficial. Good work.

Student: I was sitting on the bus one day and I had this horrendous dislike of the man sitting across from me. I felt almost revulsion. And I just looked at that feeling that has arisen; then I realized that he reminded me of someone in the past. I saw that memory, and it just dissolved.
Dr. T: Were you able to look at that man again?

Student: Yes, I did, but this time there was no more revulsion.

Dr. T: There you are. If you can shine the light of mindfulness on the mental states present, see them and know what is happening in that moment, you will exit the cycle of conditioning right then and there.

Student: It was pretty easy for me to practice. I work early in the mornings at a coffee shop, and I'm usually tired. I was able to practice watching likes and dislikes frequently, using the customers who came in as my practice; depending on who the person was and what kind of interaction I had with them. Customers can be really pleasant, and then I'll try to be pleasant with them. If they are not being nice to me, I get angry with them for not being nice. And that's where I would catch it: when I noticed my frustration with them not being nice to me, I noticed how much I disliked it. Then, during rushes, I would lose the noticing because it got too busy, and I would only realize later on that I hadn't been mindful at all.

Dr. T: The mind moves extremely fast, and your emotions have been conditioned to run wild: mindfulness can't catch up with the speed of emotions and thoughts until it can be speeded up with repeated practice. They are not running in tandem, i.e., awareness has been lagging behind. For the untrained mind, awareness is pretty sluggish and arises only when the emotions start to subside. Our expected outcome of DLMP is that mindfulness will speed up, to at least work in tandem with the emotions as they arise. If your mindfulness becomes faster than your emotions and thoughts, it will actually slow them down and perhaps stop them. The emotions will be overtaken by mindfulness.

Student: Is that what you call equanimity?

Dr. T: Yes. The emotions will subside and awareness takes over. But to get to this point, mindfulness practice has to mature and get speeded up enough to be aware of emotions and thoughts as they arise. It takes a lot of practice: it's not going to happen overnight. Or it may happen here and there, but the old conditioning is still very strong.

That's why clarifying our intention to practice, to understand why we want to practice and how to practice effectively is so important. Just keep on doing what you're doing, working in the coffee shop is good practice; constant irritation!

Student: When practicing this week, I noticed more likes, especially when I went with my family to the beach. I love to walk on the beach and swim. But I found myself getting greedy, wanting to do everything at once and it turned into impatience. I was really there to be with people, my sister and family and parents, but I found that I was greedy to get the experience of being outdoors; I wanted to do everything at once! "Come on, gotta go to the beach, hurry up and jump in the boat, so we can get back and then I want to go for a walk!"

Dr. T: That's a good way to notice how liking, wanting, and greed lead to impatience or annoyance and ill will.

My daughter was about thirteen when she came to a one-day retreat I would lead. She told me she just wanted to observe and not participate. At the end of the retreat I was cooking at home and she was studying in her room. After sometime she came out and said to me, "Mum, I can't stand Daddy's Burmese classical music. I want it to stop. How should I practice mindfulness?" I told her, "Just watch your wanting it to stop." She then went back to her room and about 10 minutes later she came out smiling broadly and said to me, "Mum that wanting it to stop is gone! But I still don't like the music." I told her, "That's fine," and she went happily back to her studies. What happened was that she was able to stop at dislike and exit the cycle and not let it progress to resentment and anger, or clinging to anger, hence avoiding verbal discord with her father.

Student: I've been successful simply noticing and going a little bit further with, "What is the cause and where did it start," as far as my likes, dislikes and reactivity. My husband took me to the beach on Saturday to get me out of the house because I've been working, a lot. I went rather reluctantly but I watched my resentment on the way. Ultimately, by the time we got to the beach I got through the dislike rather quickly. I was very relaxed and very comfortable just sitting there looking at the sand. I was able to let go of whatever the attachment was, the clinging, and was able to understand how it all began with my disliking, which then progressed to resentment. I felt very good that I could recall my mental processes going into the cycle and then exiting it.

Student: I'm learning again and again that one must practice even if one is not getting it. That's probably the American part of me, to feel like, "I'm not getting it. I had a bad practice day." But the point of the practice is that you do it, even if you don't think you've got it. You do it and trust. There is trust involved, and patience. So that's what I'm learning.

Dr. T: That's a very good insight. Americans are so goal and achievement-oriented and also conditioned to want results instantaneously. There is no patience. And if they can't get it the few first times, then they give up. Or they think, "This is not the right thing for me." In any kind of practice, you do have to persevere, you are not going to get it right away. Playing piano, swimming or tennis, everything needs practice, repetition, training and retraining the mind. Sorry there is no free ride!

Student: I think it also has to do with the fact that our American

minds are conditioned to a certain kind of greed or selfishness;
"What is it that I am going to get out of this? I have to know that
first, and then I will work my tail off to try to get there." There's no
trust that we can be guided toward positive change. Instead, we
have to know what it is and how it's going to happen, and then we
try to force it to happen!

Dr. T: You are right, without trusting the process you will never
persevere. This practice requires trusting in your innate ability, your
innate intelligence. And that's what Americans have a hard time
with, because there is so much orientation towards achievement,
there is always a standard to try to attain. And if you don't get it
right away, then just find another distraction, or another guru, or
another group. But what you are doing here is just becoming aware
of your mental processes. It's not a competition. We just want to
see how your mind functions in your daily life. How you get caught
up with things. From dislike, one of you said you could watch it
subside, but also sometimes you'd get caught up in the
consequences of dislikes. That's all we want to do. We're not
intending right now to abolish all your dislikes and keep all your
likes: you can't do that either. Even the dislikes that continue to
generate other things, where are they now, right now?

Class: Not here anymore.

Dr. T: Right, they exist only when they exist and then they are gone.

Student: I feel that this is really the nitty-gritty of the practice. What you are saying is really the truth. I was feeling so discouraged because I wasn't practicing, I wasn't doing practice as much as I thought I should.

Dr. T: It takes time for the practice to kick in; but once it takes hold, it becomes second nature. It is second nature, or even "first nature," because you are using the mental factors of mindfulness, peacefulness, and curiosity that you already possess.

For the next two weeks, practice recognizing your likes and dislikes throughout the day, Notice when you are feeling uncomfortable, angry, unhappy or especially happy; sure signs that you're either liking something or pushing something away. Try and keep a record of your likes and dislike in the sheet provided so you can look back and see how likes and dislikes run your life.

CHAPTER SIX: JUDGMENTS

This chapter is about how to practice mindfulness on one of the most difficult mind states in our daily life that usually leads to suffering in ourselves and others, i.e., judgments. Judgments are based on our perceptions and are very subjective and personal. They are based on our past experience and memories, through which we develop filters, which, in turn, usually color how we see the world. How we choose to react to everything we come in contact with results from these filters. For practical purposes let's look at the Cycle of Conditioning again.

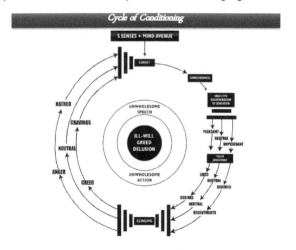

Diagram 6.1: The Cycle of Conditioning

In the cycle we see that judgment comes after our discrimination of sensations or our sensory experiences. When we experience a sensation of pleasure we respond as, "This is wonderful, I love it, I want more of it," on the other hand when we experience sensation as painful we respond as." This is awful, unjust, why me, this is unacceptable, etc." The series of responses either through pleasure or pain is based on our value system and we judge these experiences through our personal values. In our practice we call these value judgments.

Value judgments are not static. This means we don't just stay with our value judgments we let them rule how we respond to people, things, events and our environment. For example; during one of my regular classes I handed a rotten apple to the class and asked each student to handle it and look at it.

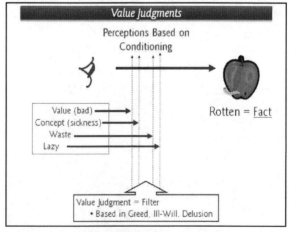

Diagram 6.2: Value Judgments

Their responses were varied:
Yuck, it looks awful. I wouldn't eat it.

I can still cut off the bad part and eat the rest.

It looks moldy. I am afraid to touch it.

It will be good for composting.

I feel sick when I look at it because when I was young I
bit into an apple and there was a worm in it.

We can see that a rotten apple by itself is just a rotten apple, but it creates a different response in different people based on their past experience and the value system they espouse. To an organic gardener, it is a useful and welcome item. To a person who already has a fungal infection, it provokes fear. To another person it brings back very unpleasant childhood memories and it made that person sick just by looking at it. The rest of our responses follow from this initial and immediate response. This happens very fast and before we can say Jack Robinson we are either loving the apple, or the experience, or hating it and we are well into the Cycle of Conditioning.

Our value judgments either provoke like, dislike or neutral. If dislike happens, it in turn, provokes resentment and when resentment intensifies it leads to anger, hatred and rage and so on. When liking happens we create desire, grasping, clinging, and obsession. Both reactions end up in the Cycle of Conditioning or

Suffering.

I can't emphasize enough that value judgment is the single, most critical, juncture on the Cycle of Conditioning. It keeps the wheel of suffering running on and on, leading to self judgment, pity, guilt, rage, discord and conflict with others, or obsession.

Then we ask, "How can we not judge anything?" "How do we function in life without judgment?" Here we need to differentiate between Value Judgment (VJ) and Factual Discernment (FD). Let me talk about both of these. Value judgment, as I mentioned earlier, is based very much upon our belief system as well as our past experiences and memories.

Factual discernment is seeing things as they are in the present moment without superimposing value judgments, which can be many layered. In the case of the rotten apple, if we can remove all the filters of personal values and past memories we will see the rotten apple as just a rotten apple, pure and simple (that is factual discernment).

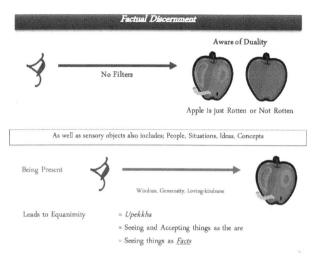

Diagram 6.3: Factual Discernment

Yes, it is rotten and now what? We can take it just as it is without any of the attendant emotions or create any of the drama around it. If we want to eat it, we cut off the bad part and just eat it. If we want to compost it, we just throw it into the compost pile. If we are not sure about mold we can throw it into the garbage. And even if we remember the apple-eating worm of our childhood we can discern factually that this apple is in the present and there may or may not be a worm inside.

One cannot exist without the other. Then we ask, "How do we deal with duality?" Do we choose the midpoint of the spectrum? I would say not. If we choose the midpoint we are still caught in the value system. It is extremely difficult to find that midpoint in any of our value systems. Allegorically speaking, even if we can find the midpoint we will still be fixated about it.

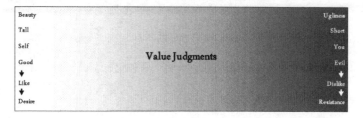

Diagram 6.4: Duality Spectrum

Then what do we do? What we have to do as a practice of mindfulness is to recognize our filters or value judgments as they occur. Once we recognize them we then have to transcend them like peeling off layers of an onion. When we can see things as they truly are, then we can decide which value judgment is going to be beneficial for us.

Example

I was teaching a one-day retreat in Scarsdale, NY, at one of my friend's/student's home. For lunch, we each brought our own bag lunch. I brought two of what I thought were veggie patties in case someone did not bring lunch. After lunch, we had a discussion and everyone reported their experience during lunch time.

One friend who was in the kitchen heating the soup reported first. She said, "I was stirring the soup and somebody needed a pan to heat a chicken patty so I found what I thought was the right pan and just gave it to her. Just then, Jain came into the kitchen and when she saw the cover of her best ceramic pot being used as a frying pan she was startled and tried to retrieve it and replace it with a frying pan. I felt very bad but I tried watching my discomfort and the discomfort faded away. And it was okay."

And then Jain, the lady of the house said, "As soon as I saw that they were using the ceramic cover of my best pot as a frying pan, I felt annoyed and blurted out something like, "That's the cover of my ceramic pot not a frying pan!" I suppose my comments put everybody off because Pam immediately replaced the cover with a frying pan and I also felt there was tension in the kitchen after my outburst. I felt so bad. I thought, "I'm being a very bad hostess. I felt I was rude. It's only a ceramic cover anyway."

The young lady whose patty was the center of attention said, "It was my chicken patty so when Jain came in and said what she said, I felt like wanting to disappear from the scene. It brought up an old memory from my childhood. My mother would always shoo me out of the kitchen so I've always felt that I am not welcome in the kitchen. And then to make matters worse, another memory arose. I was at a Zen center at a retreat. My job was to wash dishes. I broke a beautiful bone china teacup and was severely reprimanded. All those memories crowded in, in that moment. So that chicken patty created a lot of suffering for me."

One can see that the same chicken patty invoked different reactions to different people depending on their own memories of the past and various filters of value judgments of themselves, along with fears and frustrations. If everyone were able to see that the chicken patty was simply being cooked in the wrong utensil, there would have been no emotional reactions to it. It would have been just a matter of fact. But it was a good example of how our personal filters set up a different chain of reaction in each person.

Then there was another intensive I taught in Nyack, also in New York. We rented a place from a non-profit organization. There were about 12 or 13 of us. Part of the group was to cook while watching their mind states as part of the practice. Another group's task was just to clean up. After lunch, the whole group met again and we held our discussion session. In the cooking group was a young college student who said that when she went into the kitchen and everyone from the other group kept piling into it, it caused her to have a strong resentment. She thought, "The kitchen now belongs to us, the cooking group, why is the cleaning group also here?" Then she thought, "What are they doing in my kitchen?" She had never even been in that kitchen before she came to the retreat. Just because I had assigned her and her group to work in the kitchen, that became her territory for that time-period. We see here that a mere suggestion created a filter of ownership of the kitchen and caused a lot of suffering for her.

Practice

For your exercise, think of a pet peeve, one that bothers you the most. Let's look at what happens when you think of it. Do you feel a negative emotion rise up when you think about the issue? Can you discern whether the reason for your pet peeve is a value judgment or rational discernment? Take for example water dripping from a faucet that someone left on and that, for this example; this is a pet peeve of yours. Sure, on the rational level it is a waste of water, especially if it goes on for a long time. But your mind is churning, "Can't they see how wasteful it is", "can't they be more disciplined?"

Already value judgments arise leading to your own emotional discomfort.

Sometimes we can see our value judgments superimposed on our rational discernment and creating our own suffering. This does not mean that we do not do anything about it. The real difference with the practice is that we will identify what is not feasible but we will be less emotional and therefore we can deal with the situation with more clarity. If we need to ask others to be more aware of turning off the faucet we will do so or take other measures like putting a reminder in the kitchen or in the bathroom. But if it is a public place we can just turn it off and let it be.

Another exercise would be to take a look around the room you are in while reading this book. Take a few moments to notice what you feel is wrong with items in the room. Maybe the lighting is too low, the furniture is getting shabby, the color scheme is too muted, maybe there are too many knick-knacks, etc. Take notice of anything that you judge to be negative. Then try to discern whether it is a value judgment or a rational discernment. If it is a value judgment, try to peel off your negative perception of it and see what is left. For example; let's say you think the furniture is shabby. It is a fact isn't it? You can ask, "Can I be ok with that?" If not, you might have all these value judgments coming up in your mind: "Shabby is not acceptable," "Are we that poor?" and on and on. If we stop all the mental and emotional rumblings in our mind we will find that we will be left only with the fact that the furniture is shabby and it will be just the way it is and we will be none the worse for it. If it needs to be replaced, you can plan on replacing it as a matter of fact.

Experiences of Students and Discussion

Student: A friend of mine was showing me a flower petal. He said, "Look how beautiful this is." It was very translucent. It was very lovely, the light shining through it. Then he picked up an onion skin and held it up next to the flower petal. Right away I had an aversion to the onion skin because it was part of an onion. That was my first reaction. But when I looked again closely at the onion skin and really observed my reaction, I suddenly saw that it was very beautiful; the skin of the red onion. It was also very translucent just like the flower petal. In fact, it had more color to it than the flower petal and it was even more beautiful. It was very surprising to me. I was ready to just reject it because of my association with the cutting of an onion making me cry.

Dr. T: These are all the filters, or perceptions, which we harbor from the past. All of them are habitual or conditioned by our experiences. Your ideals, life story, events, your expectations, associations, etc.; color the present experience in the moment. That's how we come to see the world through a smoke screen which the Buddha called delusion.

Student: Can you explain about delusion in this?

Dr. T: The delusion we are talking about in Buddhism is about not knowing what's happening in us at the moment. The delusion is thinking what I think right now is absolute truth. For example, thinking that red onion skin is never beautiful. But upon watching and coming to realize what's happening in the mind she saw she was attached to her previous experience of cutting an onion which has nothing to do with the piece of onion skin she is looking at. Only when she let go of the memory of the past and the filter that was clouding her mind, did she begin to relate to that piece of onion skin as it was. She was able to see the beauty of it. This is how we practice mindfulness on our value judgments.

Student: I notice myself not listening or unable to pick up information whenever I have the value judgment that the subject at hand is unimportant. I have also learned that the goal of the practice is not about not having any value judgments but to use them in a skillful way. But it is really tricky to separate value judgment and factual discernment. I also realized one way to do it is to see how the value judgment affects me and others and if and how it leads to suffering; then I just use them skillfully.

Dr. T: Yes, it is true. There are value judgments that are beneficial. For example; drunk driving is unsafe, too much sugar is bad for health, exercising is the best health prevention. These are values which can be used skillfully in crucial situations. They can even be life saving.

Student: This practice on VJ has softened the edges of my thought process in my home life. I am able to quickly recognize my VJ and really change my perception of things and hence redirect my thoughts more factually which set a different tone for the whole evening with my young family.

Dr. T: Yes, the more practiced a person is in mindfulness on judgments the quicker he or she will recognize judgment in themselves. Just as soon as it arises, so the negative judgments can be prevented from continuing. We can see this in itself resulting in the transformation of our unskillful habits and bringing about harmony with our environment.

Student: The focus on the VJ vs. FD helps me re-set the place of the Cycle of Conditioning in my daily existence. In particular, it was helpful to see the way VJ "got the ball rolling" for future attachments and clinging. That reality had escaped me as of late and I can directly attribute my closely held "truths" to suffering of various kinds.

Dr. T: The important thing is to be able to realize how our VJs are hurting us and our relationships. But the conditioning is so strong it does take a lot to change our mental habits. That is why retraining the way we look at the world is so crucial on the spiritual path.

Student: VJ would appear in my mind perfectly in a child-like fashion; no sauce for the chicken nuggets? No biscuits? Of course the VJ were recognized, laughed at internally and promptly let go of. I suppose the Factual Discernment replaced or closely followed the VJ. (This was after an intensive workshop on judgments. He was able to accept things as they were at home.)

Student: My absolute value judgments make life harder for myself and others and I want my life to be easier and happier. But it is hard to control them because there is the thought that life is not black and white and there needs to be some kind of judgment to function well.

Dr. T: Yes, you are right; we do need to make judgments to function well in life. We have to make judgments according to time, place and person. For example; we cannot give too much freedom to our young children without discrimination, but we need to let them have the freedom to explore life when they are grown up.

Student: Last night it was my teenage son's turn to cook dinner. When we got home the dinner was ready, but it was cold. I was initially upset at not having a warm meal waiting. I looked at my mind and saw I was having feelings of anger and frustration and also disappointment arose. I was able to get beyond them. I also saw the factual part of the situation and was able to let it be. When I looked at it as "just a meal that happens to be cold." I was able to accept it as it was and not get annoyed at my son. It was a great opportunity to practice and look at my mind.

Student: I find it that the quicker I can get to a FD the quicker I get off the path of suffering. In that also realizing all these VJ are mostly just all about me. VJ's are an attempt to validate the "me" (shows me I exist, am important etc.) FD just is and isn't based on validating the self. And that is really freeing!!

Dr. T: I am glad you have reached a very crucial fact that VJ in most cases are all about the "self" and its validation and you realize the mind can be liberated if it is not bound up with the validation of "self" and its habitual value judgments.

CHAPTER SEVEN: CLINGING

In the last chapter we dealt with how to practice mindfulness on judgments within the Cycle of Conditioning. In this chapter we are going to discuss how the Cycle of Conditioning is repeated again and again and reflects how it is easy to slip into that groove in our mind. This is exactly how mental, verbal and physical habits are formed and constitute what we call personality or in Buddhist terms habitual kamma*.

Let's look at the Cycle again:

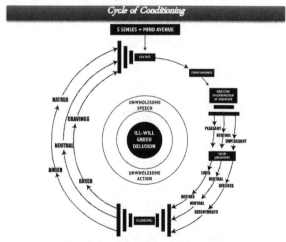

Diagram 7.1: The Cycle of Conditioning

You will see that clinging is depicted at the bottom of the cycle. This position denotes the fact that when desire intensifies as craving it results in grasping or clinging. Note that clinging can happen at any stage in the cycle, beginning particularly at the point of sense pleasures and value judgments. This is happening within the cycle which means the mind is caught in a web of its own creation.

THE ORDER OF PERCEPTABILITY
IN MINDFULNESS PRACTICE

Diagram 7.2: The Order of Perceptibility

In general, this is applicable to all things in life and the Buddha described the three major areas that, as humans, we cling to very easily:

1. All things in the sense world

2. Existence

3. Non-existence

Everything in the sense world can be clung to. Besides clinging to other human beings this includes; animals, inanimate objects, and abstract thoughts such as power, doctrine, religion, politics, society, gender, science, art, music, fame, success, or even failure, etc.

Existence means clinging to life and as such death becomes very scary and threatening. At a more subtle level we cling to all our own likes, dislikes and judgments because they seem to make us feel alive at a subtle existential level.

Sometimes, when life is too difficult to bear, people very commonly feel they want to exit this life of deep suffering. At the subtle level it would seem as if we will not exist if we have to relinquish our likes, dislikes and judgments. Of course, according to Buddhist teaching, all of this is an illusion of the mind because of its inherent insecurity and our need to cling to our emotions as a way of substantiating our existence.

Exercise on Cravings

Let's try this exercise with something that you really crave; like coffee, chocolate, or ice cream. Start tasting it and be mindful, as you are eating or drinking, of how you are enjoying it. Next, let's stop the process of eating and drinking for a while. Can you see how you want the next bite, the next spoonful? Now suppose you put away the chocolate or ice cream and take time to sit down for a few minutes and see how you feel. Do you still want to enjoy them? If you do, can you look at what it is you are yearning for? The ice cream is gone, the chocolate too. But you remember the taste of what you just had and want more of it. If you can't resist and have to go back and get the ice cream then it shows you are still clinging to the ice cream. If you can let the ice cream and the memory of ice cream "be", then you have already let go.

A beautiful sunset... Ah, I wish I could stay here forever. Ice cream... I finished a tub but it is so delicious I want some more. My girlfriend has left me and it has been hell for me. These are all states of suffering as we cling to the people, objects, or even sunsets, because we want to enjoy the sense experience again and again. Actually, what we are doing is clinging to the memory of these things and craving to repeat the sense experience of it. In other words we want to indulge in the senses connected to these things. It is also very seductive to live on these memories but the longing to have it again is what we cling to. When our clinging is too strong, we suffer when we cannot get what we want or our wish is not fulfilled. The more ardent our want or need is the more severe our suffering. Or if the clinging is excessive then it leads to addiction and obsession.

How to Practice Mindfulness on Clinging

Like all mindfulness meditations, we have to watch the clinging like a witness and not allow discursive thinking to happen around the clinging.

At first, it may be very hard to even discern our clinging if our craving, fear, or emotional states are very strong. Then it is helpful to be mindful of the craving until it is lessened and then try to watch the clinging. A lot of times it is buried beneath emotions like jealousy, fear, anxiety, pride.

Let me give you an example of how you can watch your clinging. Suppose you look at your open hand with your fingers spread out. Look at whatever is beyond the fingers. You will see that you can detect anything present beyond the fingers. You will go beyond the fingers and see what is behind it. Similarly you can go beyond your feelings of fear and anxiety and detect your clinging. Once you see clinging and watch it, again and again, it will be no more. It will be replaced by the watching mind. But, if it is a very chronic case of clinging then it may take much longer and your progress will also depend on how strong your mindfulness has become.

Three strikes. One clue as to whether you are clinging or not is to watch whatever emotions you are having; anxiety, fear, irritation, etc. and go back to it three times, and if the emotion does not resolve then you can be sure there is clinging behind these emotions. You can then use the finger method to discern the clinging. Once you see the clinging, it is of upmost importance to just watch it mindfully without any discursive thinking much like the way you would watch your breath in the silent sitting meditation practice. In this case, you are instead watching your clinging as your object of mindfulness. As you keep watching it, the clinging will be replaced by your act of watching it and the mind will just let go. You will not need to try to let go of the clinging.

Discussion with Students

Jay: I find it very difficult to let go.

Dr. T: Yes, it is difficult to let go because you cannot practice letting go.

Jay: Why?

Dr. T: Because letting go is the result of clinging. It's an effect not the cause of suffering. You can only practice on the cause which is clinging. Once the cause is removed letting go happens as a sequel.

Jay: Is all clinging "bad?" Aren't there situations where we do need to cling?

Dr. T: I think we need to clarify between desire and clinging. Desire by itself according to *Abhidhamma** or Buddhist Psychology and Philosophy is neither good nor bad but when it combines with certain feelings like grasping or greed then it becomes unwholesome.

For example; desire for spiritual development is a noble desire called Samma Chanda* or Noble Desire. But if this desire for one's own salvation becomes an extreme grasping of the goal, it only obstructs one's path. It's the same with the desire for children to grow up and have a good life. This is a noble desire but if we cling or grasp on to our ideas and become obsessed with them that's when we suffer, especially if our desire is not fulfilled. Or the desire to have a good sound healthy relationship with one's spouse or partner is a noble desire but when that desire becomes craving it tends to lead to clinging and that usually becomes harmful in a relationship.

Dr. T: I have a friend who goes on retreat very frequently. One day she called me up and said, "I am very upset because I was planning on going on this retreat and family affairs have been deterring me from going." So I asked her, "Why do you go to retreats?" She said, "I wanted to reduce my defilements." I asked,

"What's happening to you right now?"

She replied, "Oh yes, I am having more defilements right now."

That night, she later told me, as she sat in meditation; she felt a curtain lifting in her mind. For most of us it is really difficult to discern at what point our desire goes on to become craving. Then clinging is very difficult to discern because the transition from desire to grasping is so subtle. We usually miss it because it is almost instantaneous.

It's like the razor's edge. As humans we tend to rationalize all our needs in a way that is more self-serving than not. Because of this, before long we slip into clinging without realizing what had happened. It can happen in the flicker of an eyelid and we can get caught in the trap of clinging, completely unaware. Then we pursue our target in usually unwholesome ways because clinging comes from the ego and also feeds into ego. Before long it becomes a tug of war or power play between individuals. That's how a lot of suffering happens in us and this is what is called the awakened state. That is also the way the untrained mind functions.

Jay: So in the mindfulness practice, just watching our clinging is going to help us untangle ourselves from it?

Dr. T: Yes, but you have to be able to see your clinging first because it is usually hidden underneath other emotional states. For example; we are annoyed with someone and we cannot stop being annoyed with them for a long time. We do not notice the underlying clinging to the annoyance. We are aware only of our annoyance so even if we watch annoyance it may still come back because we have not dealt with the clinging, which is usually to the memory of the annoyance. The memories serve as a stimulant and they provokes us every time we think about the incident or the person. So in mindfulness practice it is very crucial to see your clinging and not get focused on the memories of the incident or the person. If we keep thinking about the memories it will just keep on provoking more emotions and we will miss out on our mind state of clinging to the memories or the need to indulge in the pleasure of the memories.

Mel: I definitely cling to my judgments of my son. I am constantly judging him to my standards (in my head) and clinging to how he should be. How should I deal with my clinging?

Dr. T: Well, here you are clinging to judging him according to your standards so you are clinging to two things; Judging and standards. First, you practice letting your value judgments of him be and not clinging to them. Also look at your perceived standards because they are the filters through which you look at him. When you can see how you cling to both judging and standards then the filters will drop away and you can see him as he is; as a fourteen year old who may not have the standards of behavior of his 50-year-old mom.

When my son was a teenager he came to talk to me about some problems he had with his friends. I tried to give him some suggestions and solutions but I found he was not really hearing me. I was starting to get a bit annoyed but suddenly my thoughts dropped away and I saw I was clinging to my own perception of myself as "The mother who knows it all." Of course he was not hearing me, because my mind was not free. It was full of this "Big Mother" image. Once the clinging to this image dropped away I could really see his suffering, only then.

Mel: What did you do then?

Dr. T: I stopped talking and was just very present with him. I found he was pouring his heart out and I felt a shift happening between us. I can't exactly remember what we talked about but there was just this connection between us that was just lovely and he was also content for the rest of the night.

Mel: Aren't there certain areas of your life that that are necessary to cling to?

Dr. T: Sure there are certain instances or areas we need to hold on to. For example; you could hold on to the safety of your children, to the safety of your house, driving safely, or some crucial problem-solving. For instance, I have some health problems. The most debilitating one is a very unstable pelvis. Because of this, I was unable to walk without severe pain in my legs. It took me about five years to get the right kind of treatment. You could say I held on to finding the solution to my physical problem. I would not leave any stone unturned. You might call it perseverance, but there is still some holding on, or clinging, to finding a solution.

Finally I found the right kinds of treatment and my life is so much better now. It's the same with safe driving. I would insist that people don't talk too much or argue when I ride with another. This is really dangerous. Sure I was clinging to the idea but it saves lives and avoids accidents. Again we use factual thinking in these circumstances and determine what is best for us. What serves me as well as the others at the same time? The only difference is that we have to be careful not to let clinging go too far and end up with obsession or perfectionism.

Mel: How do you deal with obsessive clinging or clinging to being perfect?

Dr. T: It depends on how serious it is. I was teaching a retreat in Nevada City many years ago and participants asked me what delusion is. I asked the group, "How many of you are perfectionists?" and almost all of them raised their hands. I followed, "Is there such a thing as perfection?" All of them laughed. I then explained, "Then that's delusion, isn't it?"

We are just clinging to the delusion that we can be perfect or should be perfect. No matter what we cling to, the moment we let our minds grasp on to it we unwittingly let the clinging wrap our minds up in it and it's really hard to discern the clinging itself.

CHAPTER EIGHT: THE PATH OF WISDOM

The most frequent question asked by some of my Western Dhamma* teacher friends is how insight arises in the Daily Life Mindfulness Practice (DLMP). It is common knowledge that in the silent, sitting meditation model, Vipassana or meditative insights, arise mostly during deep meditative states. DLMP however does not provide opportunities for deep meditative states to arise as we have to move about almost constantly throughout the day. But this does not mean that meditative insights do not arise at all for DLMP practitioners. They do arise but in a very different way. The insights in daily life arise in the context of the situation that the practitioner is in; not as the insights of phenomena at their microscopic level as in the silent sitting.

The main qualities of mind that will be developed through DLMP are equanimity and balance. Equanimity will bring the emotions to a calmer and more steadfast place and will enable the person to find equilibrium amidst the ups and downs of living. This brings the mind to a state of spaciousness and that is when insight and wisdom will unfold in a manner to give us a better handle on our day to day problems. If the mind is too preoccupied with discursive thinking and a lot of negative emotions there is practically no chance for insights to arise.

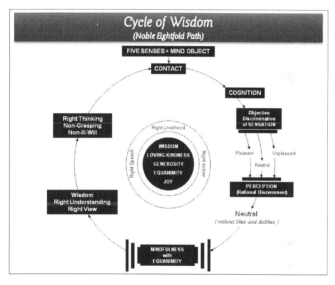

Diagram 8.1: Cycle of Wisdom

Many years ago, one of my students almost experienced a typical situation of road rage. He was driving on a side road and another car was driving on the main road. They were racing against each other to reach the intersection where the two roads were to meet; and both were getting angry. In the midst of it the man who was my student found his anger dropped away all of a sudden and he immediately saw how stupid he was in trying to race the other car. He saw he was in the wrong and yet was trying to beat the other car. He laughed at his own folly and slowed down thereby avoiding a possible fatal accident. He had been studying with me for about a year, but he said he was not intentionally practicing mindfulness. The letting go of the anger happened spontaneously. Through the arising of insight or wisdom, he recognized his folly and saved himself or even the other driver from a near fatal accident.

The above "road rage" experience is a Vipassana insight or experiential insight brought about by his practice. It was not an intellectual insight but a real transcendental insight (transcending the ego.) When he was furious it was his ego and pride leading him in the road rage. The moment that his ego and pride were transcended insight simultaneously arose and he saw his folly.

When DLMP has become established to a good extent, this process of letting go of and dropping difficult emotions happens automatically. If we compare the mind to a computer, DLMP can be likened to the installation of new software into the mind. When we have practiced enough letting go through DLMP, the mind becomes conditioned to letting go of emotions at the most critical times. This is exactly like having the new software kicking in and running a new program by itself. It's just a new habit that we have "installed" into ourselves and the natural intelligence or wisdom factor (according to Buddhist psychology) of the mind does its own work even without our willing it. Such is the beauty of this practice.

In class, one of my young students reported that during an argument with her boyfriend she was tense and argumentative, but in the midst of the argument suddenly her emotions dropped away and she saw how she was feeding into the situation by her negative reactions. She was surprised to find that she also was able to see how her boyfriend was feeling and further able to understand his predicament. She commented that it was really freeing for her for the first time.

Different Levels of Insights

I. Mundane Insights

In everyday life the insights that arise are usually insights which we experience, whether we practice DLMP or not. For example, when we were in school we tried to work out a solution to a math problem but found it very hard and ultimately we stopped working on it or thinking about it. Then, after a while, maybe in the shower or getting up from bed in the morning the answer just hits us. That is mundane insight.

II. **Vipassana or Spiritual Insights**

One time one of my students was walking along a street and suddenly found that her sense of self just dropped away and she felt everything and everybody was part of her and she felt utter peace. It did not last very long but it was an experiential insight of the dropping away of the sense of self. She was not really practicing mindfulness at that moment nor was she a regular sitting meditator. It just happened spontaneously.

In another example, in the late 90's, I was teaching DLMP at a retreat in Australia. One of the participants was a woman who had never meditated before but had done Tai Chi for five years prior to the retreat. On the second day of the retreat she experienced an insight called Dissolution Insight where she saw her thoughts crumbling like sand. This happened while she was walking in the dormitory where she was staying.

Lastly, at my center in California, one of my senior students had a similar experience while he was driving home from class one evening. That night, in class, we did a small exercise of looking inwards directly into the mind for a few minutes. Afterwards, during his drive, his mind slowed and he found he was seeing a thought falling away. Usually this kind of insight occurs during deep meditative states experienced by practitioners during silent sitting retreats. But it can also occur in DLMP while functioning in everyday life and it does not interfere with how a person functions. The insight arises only for a nano-second and the person is back to their everyday mind. My student who was driving went on driving without any mishap.

When equanimity and concentration are in perfect equilibrium, as a result of constant mindfulness practice, wisdom or insight arises spontaneously. With arising of wisdom there is usually also the arising of joy and compassion.

When DLMP has become established to a good extent, this process of letting go of and dropping difficult emotions happens automatically. If we compare the mind to a computer, DLMP can be likened to the installation of new software into the mind. When we have practiced enough letting go through DLMP, the mind becomes conditioned to letting go of emotions at the most critical times. This is exactly like having the new software kicking in and running a new program by itself. It's just a new habit that we have "installed" into ourselves and the natural intelligence or wisdom factor (according to Buddhist psychology) of the mind does its own work even without our willing it.

III. Incredible Natural Intelligence (Wisdom)

In Abhidhamma*, or Buddhist Psychology and Philosophical teachings, the Buddha describes the 52 mental factors. One of them is the wisdom faculty. This faculty arises only when there is mindfulness and equanimity in the moment. It never arises when the mind is chock-full of anger, doubt, fear, irritation, or any of the whole gamut of defiled negative states. These negative unwholesome states cannot arise in the same moment as the wholesome mind states like wisdom, joy and compassion. They can exist in alternation but they never occur simultaneously. So the more our mental states are in the wholesome mode, the better is the chance for insight/wisdom to arise. This, in turn, conditions us to be a better person in many aspects and brings forth peace and harmony within oneself and in ones connection with others.

We each have this natural wisdom aspect in us because we were born with it. We can see proof of this in children. At times, this wisdom surprisingly unfolds in them even without their ever practicing meditation. When my son was about eight years old, one day he lost playing monopoly with his sister and her friends. He was very upset and left the game. I tried to pacify him by saying it is only a game and so on. I found he was not really hearing me but suddenly he piped up saying, "Mom, why is it I don't get angry when I play with toys but only when I play with money?"

He meant play money, but even then the connotation of money was powerful to him and he recognized it. That was an intuitive, natural intelligence or insight, that each of us are born with. Yet it arises only when the circumstances are right. In DLMP we are intentionally training our mind to create such appropriate circumstances within us so that this kind of intuitive natural wisdom has a better chance of arising to lead us to live a life of creative intelligence and harmony.

CHAPTER NINE:
THE PATH OF THE HOUSEHOLDER

Nearly forty years ago, in Burma, I had the good fortune to study with two Burmese Abbots. They taught the DLMP without any sitting practice at a time when the silent sitting meditation was all the rage in Burma. I was very attracted to their teaching because their approach was very down to earth and pragmatic especially for householders. I remember them saying to us, "Don't come to us because of heart breaks or when your business collapses. This monastery is not a place of escape from the travails of your life. But we can teach you how to face life and function in the everyday world as a liberated human being." And they actually walked their talk. After studying with them closely for just eight months my life took many turns, and for forty years their teaching and the DLMP has held me in good stead as I have negotiated many turmoil's; as a householder, as a wife, a mother and with my career. Being able to walk and not waver was a great gift from my two teachers.

When I was working as a physician, I was asked by other physicians, mostly Americans, how the Dhamma and the Daily Life Mindfulness Practice (DLMP) affected my life as a physician. I found there was a very dramatic shift in my perception as a professional woman even while I was studying with my two teachers in the early part of the 1970's. There was more clarity in everything I was doing and there was also a reduced sense of fear in everyday dealings in the professional arena. I became more open to ideas, to people and to life itself. I was still single then and when I decided to marry I went to my teachers and told them my decision. Contrary to most Burmese abbots they were very happy about it and said I was now being in accord with life itself and they blessed my decision. I thought that was extraordinary and to me they were being very Tao. It was also their attitude towards householder's life that steered me on to be fearless and to face life as it unfolds.

It was also through my life as a professional and householder that I had honed my own practice and developed my own way of refining and deepening it through all the difficult incidences of my life as a wife and a mother. It was through my own practice that I have been teaching my students the DLMP and fashioning it in a way that will speak to the Western householder and detail it to meet their needs as they live their lives, move through their career, raise their children, and face the myriad of other challenges of living a modern Western lifestyle. That is what I love about teaching here in America. I can bring all my past experiences as a householder and fashion it in a way to help the busy American householder to use the practice in their lives without having to leave their children and spouse to study and practice. They can practice right there in their work, their homes, during their commute, interacting with their extended families, on vacation, and everywhere else. The thing most of them like is that they don't have to take the zafu with them everywhere and still they can practice mindfulness.

When I first arrived in America and started teaching, one of my students asked me what benefit I felt I got from DLMP. I said simply "It brought me sanity." They all laughed. But it was true and still is. Imagine a fifty-year-old Burmese woman arriving in Scarsdale, New York with two teenagers and a husband who had to commute to the city to work. Becoming a soccer mom overnight, and virtually the cook, driver, maid and what have you. I am talking about a very spoiled professional Burmese woman who was pampered all her life and never lifted a finger to do any housework. I was also transitioning through menopause as well as had an inner ear problem that produced severe vertigo. It was nightmarish to say the least. But the practice supported me through thick and thin and also supported my daughter when she went through traumatic experiences of entering a high-pressure middle school in Scarsdale. In six months time she was asking me to teach her mindfulness so that she could go through the difficult adjustment.

The ups and downs in family life is a great opportunity to practice DLMP because the situation is real and immediate and you are right there in the midst of conflicts, confusions and crises big and small and you cannot run away. You have to develop enough samadhi or groundedness in the moment so that you are not thrown off your horse, so to say. You have to be steadfast enough not to buckle under the pressure and also have enough equanimity not to be sucked into the drama of family life. That brings us into the issue of how to develop Samadhi in everyday life.

Samadhi in Everyday Life

Since things are very fluid in everyday life, one cannot expect to develop the kind of deep Samadhi or one-pointed concentration that is experienced in the sitting practice. You do not have the same silence and control. But there is something called Adi-samadhi* or Khanika-samadhi (momentary concentration) in Buddhism whereby the mind can become steadfast in a single moment if practiced in the right way. This happens in daily life when we can turn our attention inwards focusing on our thoughts and emotions; there is a collectedness of attention in that moment. Even if it happens only for a few moments, it is sufficient to keep the mind very steadfast with consistent practicing. You may not hold it for very long as you have to move through your day but every time you turn your mind inwards to discern what is happening within, there is already a moment of Samadhi. A constant practice is of course necessary for this Samadhi to be a constant occurrence in the mind and will also become a built-in Samadhi state as time goes on. When that happens, you naturally become very grounded in the moment. It is a new conditioned state whereby you move through the day in a more balanced way. But, of course, there will be times when things are rough and you may falter. In those moments, you need to exert more effort to stay grounded. The way my students learn to do that is to stay very centered in themselves and to be very present to whatever is happening to them and their surroundings. From this centered state they are able to prevent themselves from getting sucked into the chaos that they are experiencing and to stay very focused.

One of my students told me about being confronted by another resident of the Center. She said she would usually react to him with fear and negativity because of past conflicts with him. But this particular time she started to stay very present with him and just focused on what he was saying and didn't let the past memories crowd in. She found she was able to interact with him without fear and negativity.

Equanimity and Indifference

One may ask with equanimity isn't there indifference? Not really, if the state of equanimity is real and complete. Complete in the sense that it is not merely suppressing one's likes and dislikes and clinging. When equanimity is real it will draw upon wisdom, compassion and loving-kindness in a way where there is no question of indifference at all. But, of course, there will be times before equanimity develops there can be indifference arising from neutrality. We have to be very vigilant then to investigate and examine whether we are truly equanimous or still being indifferent. In the case of indifference there is still a very subtle trace of resistance which is difficult to discern and may keep you from engaging freely with whatever is happening around you. With equanimity there is an openness that runs through and through. If it is true equanimity there will be wisdom that will help us from becoming codependent.

Codependency

This is the most difficult area to discern because it may be hidden from our own awareness if our motivation is to be kind but we have not really examined fully the broader perspective of any given situation. We may be fueling more suffering in another, especially when they are psychologically very needy. We may be supporting their neediness and perpetrate it instead of helping them to be truly independent. Having two adult children and teaching for thirty-some years has given me a lot of experience in sensing how much I am becoming co-dependent or how much I am supporting their dependency. Many times I have had to stop feeding their neediness through "tough love" a term which I have grown to love very much here in America. At first there will be a negative reaction from the other person and this is what we have to be prepared for, thus not caving in once we have decided not to be codependent.

The common reason why we persist in codependency is because we feel like obliging the other person every time we are asked to help. This may be because we have developed a habitual helpfulness or we are getting some self-gratification by being helpful. It is then important to discern with wisdom how to fashion the necessary boundaries, yet keep the relationship warm and kind. When we have the intention to not be codependent it is important to monitor the progress of the person becoming independent of you. If they are not making progress, then it may require that you go back to the drawing board and revise your strategy and determine where you need to change your habitual codependent tendency. If you find it difficult to change your behavior then it is time to revise and investigate whether you are in fact clinging to the self-gratification brought on by co-dependency.

All in all, it is important to keep in mind that the purpose of this process is to help both persons overcome the codependent qualities of the relationship, first and foremost, and also to let go of habitual codependent tendencies.

Compassion and Wisdom

When we are on the spiritual path it is very easy to fall into what I call the compassion trap. We can get caught in a psychological trap we create for ourselves. I have experienced it many times after I have given my children a dose of tough love. They will respond by saying, "You are a Dhamma teacher, why are you so unbending?" or "Don't you have compassion?" Such comments can lure us into a guilt trip where we can be trapped if we do not have the wisdom to resist such a compassion meltdown. The Buddha talked about how a compassionate person without wisdom is a "soft-hearted fool" and an intelligent person with no compassion is a "cold-hearted intellectual." We need to temper our compassion with wisdom. What is most important is not to react impulsively but, instead, take the time to reflect and consider what is best in the long run for ourselves and for others at the same time.

Guidelines for Living

I have been asked many times what my guidelines for living are. I have just two important guidelines from the Buddha's teaching that I have integrated into my life as a parent, as a wife, and as a Dhamma teacher; and towards whomever I come in contact with:

  a. To consider what is beneficial to me and others at the same time

  b. To not go to extremes in any situation

It is of utmost importance that my own welfare is also considered, together, with the welfare of others so that the benefits are not just for them or just for me. If that is the case then I am holding on to one extreme. If I consider myself and others at the same time, I am including myself as part of the whole; I am not isolating myself apart from others. There is no separation. If I only think of myself, then I am separating from the whole and that does not work either. If I consider only the welfare of others I am short-changing my own welfare as a human being. When we sacrifice only for others, we will feel hurt because things are at our disadvantage. To be in harmony is to stop considering oneself as the center of the universe and to be willing to be an integral part of the whole with our own humanness and needs met at the same time.

Chapter Ten:
Mindfulness on Difficult Emotions

I've been asked many times by students how to practice mindfulness with difficult emotions like anger, rage, frustrations, fear, jealousy, anxiety and so on. For beginners it may be difficult to practice mindfulness on very strong emotions like anger, emotional pain, intense physical pain, anxiety, etc. To be able to withstand the impact of these intense feelings the practitioner needs to have a very good level of concentration and groundedness and equanimity in the moment. To develop such qualities it usually takes a couple of years of DLMP. But there are some practices that can be very helpful and the following describes them:

1. Substitution
2. Mindfulness of perceptions
3. Mindfulness of first thought
4. Mindfulness directly on emotions like anger, fear
   a. to be used only by more accomplished practitioners
5. Suppressing difficult emotions

I. Substitution

When you are faced with a very challenging situation and you find your emotions are very powerful and difficult to contain, you can replace this intense state of emotion by immediately paying attention to your bodily sensations or physical activities.

Some concentration practices using the body as the object of attention can be used to at least hold the emotions in a stable manner so that they do not spill over in a drastic way. Using the breath as a stabilizing measure is very helpful here. I usually advise my students to count up to three and repeat it again and again until the emotions subside. When the emotions subside then you can watch your original difficult emotions if they have become lessened in their intensity. Then, if it is feasible, you can watch your difficult emotions until they totally resolve. If they return you may have to follow this procedure time and time again until the emotions completely dissipate.

When I was a beginner in this practice I would automatically find myself wiping the countertop again and again during a difficult crisis. You may also find some activity that helps you stabilize your emotions. Some people choose to take a quiet walk, listen to music or watch a movie; relax with a shower, a hot bath or a massage. All awhile following the sensations so that the mind is pulled away from the intense emotion. But always remember that you will need to deal with that particular emotion when it is softer and look at its beginnings, or else it will hide within and pop up through another situation.

What we want to do, as much as possible, is release it in a safe manner. This practice is based on the understanding that even the most difficult emotion is impermanent and will die down in time if left alone. Our task is to regard it like holding a baby gently. Nature will take care of it.

II. Mindfulness of Perceptions

Sometimes mindfulness on changing one's perception may be the key to exit the cycle of conditioning. Since all emotions are derived from one's perceptions, or filters, just changing from a negative filter to a positive filter can do the trick. In fact, as in our earlier mindfulness of judgment practice, when we can switch from a negative value judgment to a positive value judgment or from a negative judgment to a rational discernment then we are already out of the cycle of suffering.

During one of our beginning classes, I asked students to look at some objects in the room and to tell me what their thoughts about it. The first student picked a Burmese Buddhist ceremonial umbrella. She thought it was a lampshade. (insert photo or drawing) Here is what she said: "Well, the interesting thing that happened for me is when you said that it wasn't a lamp, that it was an umbrella, it changed my perception of it. When I first looked over at it I thought it was a lamp and I associated it with looking like a Christmas tree. I thought, 'Why would anyone want to make a lamp look like a Christmas tree?' And then, when you told me that it was a sacred umbrella, it became really beautiful. So, yeah, it did change my perception. It is interesting that I could just switch my perception and my judgment changed immediately."

Many years ago while I was teaching in Bangkok to a group of international women and men; a Swiss student talked about an encounter at her home. She was living in Thailand with her family and one day she said her husband invited a group of his business friends to lunch at their house. She recounted an accident that occurred during the visit. Her teenage son was terribly injured while he was coming down the stairs as one of the guests was going up; as they ran into one another the keys in the gentleman's hand somehow hit her son's face terribly injuring him and causing him to need stitches.

She said after that accident every time this gentleman came to their house she held a great dislike towards him and could not face him.

I asked her what her feelings were about this man before the accident. She said she did not feel friendly towards him nor did she dislike him as she did not know him well. I asked her to sit on that as a practice for the next week. When she came back to the group the next week she was all smiles and said happily, "My dislike of this man is gone!" I explained that originally she did not have any liking or disliking of this man. Her perception of him was neutral but when her son was accidentally injured by him, her perception of him changed to that of a scoundrel. But after contemplating on these facts her perception reverted back to the original state of mind; which was neutral.

III. Mindfulness of First Thought

Sometimes when an incident has passed but you are still having some problems resolving your emotions around it; it can be useful to discern what the first thought was when the incident happened. When you can discern the first thought, you may discover deeper emotions that arose with it but were not in your awareness.

One of my past students received a bill from her dentist and for some reason, got upset. She said she tried to practice mindfulness on her annoyance and it went away but it kept coming back and she asked me what she should do. I asked her what was her first thought when she saw the bill, she said, "Oh yes, my ego." She said that realization cured her annoyance.

There is a wonderful story in the Buddhist scriptures about a rabbit who was very obsessed with the fear that the sky would fall on him. One day a large fruit fell on his burrow and he ran out and started to cry, "The sky is falling! The sky is falling!" Soon all the rabbits, goats, sheep, pigs and small animals started running. Then the medium-sized animals of the forest started running creating a mass hysteria. Then the large animals joined in; the horses and cows and finally even the elephant. There was a stampede! Finally they came to a knoll where the Lion King was standing. When they saw him they all stopped and the Lion King asked them what was the matter. The elephant said it was the horse and giraffe who cried the sky was falling. The horse then turned to the deer and goats and pointed to them that they were the ones who cried the alarm. The sheep and goats then turned to the hare who cried out the alarm. So the Lion King asked the hare to take him to the place where the sky had fallen. The whole animal entourage went. When they finally got to the rabbit's burrow, they found the fallen fruit. This story is an example of how one single first thought can proliferate into a huge drama like the stampede of the animals in the forest.

IV. Mindfulness Directly on Emotions

This is not an easy practice because when emotions are strong it is hard to keep the mind grounded in the moment and watch a difficult emotion like anger or fear directly. But those who have achieved some level of grounding, or Samadhi, and equanimity may be able to just watch the anger or fear and let it be.

The important thing in this practice is to use the four basic practices prescribed in this book to watch the anger in the moment and just be present to it. The watching also needs to be without likes and dislikes, value judgments on oneself, or clinging to the person or incident that brought about anger. It would be purely watching the anger like you would watch your breath in the silent sitting practice. In short, anger becomes your object of meditation. Likewise, any other emotions can be practiced within the same way; be it fear, frustration, and so on. As you watch your emotions, try staying with them with bare attention and keep on watching. You will invariably see changes happening in the emotional state. It will soften gradually and you will find yourself distancing from it. This is a good sign that you are doing well.

There is one thing that is crucial with this practice. That is to not think around the anger. One single thought about the anger or what brought on the anger and you will lose the practice and be swept away by an internal tidal wave of guilt, frustrations, blame, etc. and it will take you away from the anger itself. You may slip into a vicious cycle of conditioning again and again. To prevent going into the loop, it is very important to just stay focused on the anger and let it be. Neither engage in it nor interrupt it. If you engage in the how and whys of the anger you will be adding fuel to the fire. If you try to stop the anger forcefully you will be frustrated because you will have only added another layer of anger. Neither of these two methods will work.

The practice involves just keeping bare attention on the anger in a similar way to how we practice mindfulness on the breath. Then the anger will live out its life span and die down eventually. But you will find it's the waiting that is difficult because it requires a lot of patience to let our difficult emotions subside by themselves.

V. Suppressing Difficult Emotions

Generally I would not advise the use of this practice but there may be times when you simply cannot express your anger or frustration. For example, in front of a boss, or young children, or someone who has a tendency towards violence. You may have to suppress your emotions temporarily until a time arrives that is more conducive to dealing with your difficult emotions through the practice. This practice should not become a habit and is not recommended unless if it is really called for.

GLOSSARY OF PALI TERMS

Abhidhamma: the third cannon of Theravada Buddhism and is the most important teachings of the mind and matter in great detail. It is also called the science of the mind.

Adi-Samadhi: momentary concentration

Dhamma: generally as teachings of the Buddha

Kamma: as the fruition of one's action in thought, word and deed

Khanika Samadhi: momentary concentrated mind

Panna: transcendental wisdom

Samma Chanda: noble desires

Sayadaw: an honorific term for monks in the Theravada tradition

Suttra: one of the three canons of Theravada scripture. It's a collection of discourses uttered by Buddha during his life time as the Buddha

Theravadan: derived from Theravada Buddhism the Southern Buddhist school which is prevalent in Burma, Sri Lanka, Thailand, Laos and Cambodia

ABOUT THE AUTHOR

Dr. Thynn Thynn is a retired physician and mother of two adult children. She has been teaching Mindfulness Meditation in everyday life for the past thirty years in Thailand and within the United States. This is her second book and it is written as a manual for those who want to practice mindfulness in their everyday life without having to leave home. She has founded the Sae Taw Win II Dhamma Center in Graton/ Sebastopol, CA area since 1998. The materials in this book are based on her hands-on- training of her classes at the Dhamma Center.

Dr. Thynn Thynn's well appreciated first book, "Living Meditation: Living Insight" was self published in 1992. It became translated into Dutch, Vietnamese, German, Chinese and Spanish. To date over 40,000 copies have been printed.